# Ways To Teach Children

BY IRIS V. CULLY

ILLUSTRATED BY HARRY EABY

FORTRESS PRESS • *Philadelphia*

# Ways To Teach Children

# Contents

# 1. The Importance of Methods

EVERYTHING a teacher does in a class involves methods. This is something you take for granted. It is a startling experience, however, to sit down and try to recall exactly what went on in a specific class session. You will immediately observe that some of the methods used were planned; others simply developed. A teacher does not always realize this.

For example, several boys and girls arrive in the church school room ahead of the teacher. They begin drawing spaceships on the blackboard, or they see a few sheets of paper lying on a table and begin a game of tic-tac-toe. This is a pre-session activity, spontaneously engaged in by children in order to take up time until something else occurs. Both the activity and the purpose derive from the immediate need of the early-comers. The teacher might anticipate the need for something to do upon arrival, and deliberately plan the activity. Books might be placed invitingly on a table for exploration, uncompleted work left in a conspicuous place, or a note written on the board: "Will early-comers please arrange the bulletin board!" Thus, directions are provided for a class when the teacher cannot arrive before the first child does.

A similar unplanned (but usually anticipated) situation arises when one child interrupts a discussion in a way that seems to the teacher to be completely off the subject. Shall the digression be ignored? Or has it been sparked in some way by the subject under consideration? Even the methods used for the discipline of the class or of an individual must be seen as a part of the total impact of a class situation. Sometimes a happening outside may determine what will happen in the class—coming to church school in a snowstorm; a child's announcement of the arrival of a new brother; the introduction of a new child or visitor into the class.

Method is everything which a teacher does to teach and through which a pupil learns. Methods are ways of communication. This does not mean that the pupil will always respond. All teachers know that often there will be no obvious response whatever. But, hopefully, there may be an inner response of which the teacher has no inkling.

The whole idea of communication as meaningful interaction has been so fully explored in other books that there is no need to go into it at length here. A reminder is in order at the beginning of a study of methods, however, that communication involves more than action on the part of the teacher alone. It is only completed by the response of the pupil. The teacher attempts to teach; but whether or not the pupil learns is due to many factors. A complete teaching-learning process may be characterized as communication.

The teacher has the option of deliberately planning methods or of drifting into them. Wondering "What shall we do today?" could lead to creative developments at the direction of a skilled and experienced teacher. It could also lead to indecision and chaos. Meditating on methods as one comes to class can be similarly fraught with danger. The wise teacher keeps in mind the objectives of the unit and then thinks of all the possibilities for appropriate methods— whether planned or spontaneous, initiated by teachers or pupils. Then he is not disconcerted by what he finds developing among the children and has a certain assurance in guiding the transition from one method to another.

Each teaching unit begins with several objectives. The methods suggested in the session plans which follow are designed to lead toward the objectives. Everything that happens in a session will help to accomplish this, or will go contrary to the objectives, or may simply ignore them. For example, it is possible to get too involved in the latest archaeological findings, or in a blow-by-blow description of the destruction of Canaan, and ignore the way in which this event is considered to be the self-disclosure of God.

Or perhaps an objective of the unit is to help the pupil to become more conscious of and responsible in his own covenant relationship with God. To some teachers, the effort to work with boys and girls in depth, helping them to be-

9

come aware of their own relationship to God, seems too difficult even to attempt. Their own faith may be weak or they may feel awkward in trying to discuss the growth of faith. So they fail to use methods which would help to explore this objective, such as discussion, an open-ended story, a comparison to the biblical situation and to our situation. Instead, they concentrate on exciting historical events which occurred thousands of years ago—and do not fulfill an important objective.

Not every unit objective has to be met in each session, but the teacher needs always to be aware of the three directions in which the units move: the events, God's actions in those events, and the meaning for us. Since methods are the way of communication, how well they are chosen and used determines how well the objectives are met.

## Method in Everything

Methods do not consist only in what a teacher does during a session. The way in which he sets the stage, as it were, is essential. Yet it is surprising how many teachers seem quite unconscious of this element in their work. One can glance in the rooms of any church school during a casual weekday visit, and observe which teachers use the surroundings as a part of their methods and which are ignoring their possibilities.

Visual methods are one category of methods. Most public school rooms are filled with evidence of the use of visual methods. There are maps and charts, displays of pupils' work, bulletin boards, chalkboards, art exhibits, display cabinets, and bookshelves. The skillful church school teacher takes a cue here. What does the child see when he enters for his Sunday, weekday or vacation church school class? Are the chairs in rows, a circle, or a semicircle? Or are they grouped around a table? Where will the teacher sit (his position indicates what he wants his role to be)? Does he stand in front of the group, sit in the middle, or at the end of the table? Are the furnishings so arranged as to give a restful, uncluttered look to the room? Even a small room, as every woman knows, can be made to look less crowded by the skillful arrangement of its contents, and by throwing out everything nonessential. Attractively painted walls and furniture, and brightly decorated windows invite the child to feel warmth and pleasure in a place thoughtfully prepared for him.

It should also be observed that equipment and materials are a part of the use of method. Filmstrips or slides obviously cannot be used unless the projector is near at hand, set up and ready to go. Graphic expression will be the same old crayon-and-paper routine unless a teacher thinks to prepare paints or provide special materials. Teachers may unnecessarily limit variety of their methods because they do not take the trouble to plan ahead, try out new equipment and materials, and show the boys and girls how to expand skills. Discriminating teaching requires that the teacher ask what specific methods will be best in a particular situation, or what form of expression can best convey the pupils' learning. Teacher's guides give guidance here.

The relationships among the persons in the class constitute another element in method. Pupils are persons and not things, and a method cannot legitimately be used "on" them or even with them without a sensitivity as to their possible response. A child's response to a method may be his response to the teacher. The teacher says, "Now we shall all draw the story as we remember it." But Tommy says, "No, I won't," or somewhat evasively, "I don't feel like drawing," or even "I can't draw that." He may be resenting the tone of voice in which the teacher spoke, or the teacher's assumption that everybody will do as told in the same way at the same time. He may be protesting boredom or the length of the session. He is not feeling receptive to either the teacher or the class session, and this conditions his response to a specific suggestion. The child who likes his teacher is eager to try to fulfill expectations made of him. A class in which boys and girls feel a mutual sense of comradeship works well together and accomplishes much.

For the relationships among the children themselves are another factor here. This may be no problem in a town or neighborhood in which all the children attend the same public school. But if they come together only on Sunday mornings (and even for an additional weekday session), and spend most of their time with children from several schools and different neighborhoods, they may have little feeling for one another. The situation can be even more acute if most of the boys and girls come from one school and only a few come from outside. The fellowship of the church or our oneness as baptized Christians can be only a formal assertion unless a class, too, senses a certain unity with one another. Bringing them together into such a unity both requires a method and becomes a method for furthering the objectives of the church for the growing child. He cannot know himself to be a part of the Christian community if he is unaccepted in his small class or if he excludes others from his circle of friends.

The relationship of the whole church to the children is another factor to be taken into consideration. Boys and girls are sensitive to the feelings of adults toward them. Their room speaks to them of the concern, or lack of concern, of the congregation toward the children. It is not necessary that everything be done to make the church school up-to-the-minute, but only that the resources of the parish shall be shared equally with reference to the needs of the children and those of the adults. A teacher is hampered in the range of methods available to him if the unconcern of the parish forces him to try to teach with minimum equipment in unsatisfactory space. The children can hardly grasp the fact that the church is the family of God when they feel treated as if they were an afterthought, a necessary but hardly welcome adjunct. This happens occasionally in a church with predominantly older members, or in a congregation busy with many activities. The wholeness of the community of faith must be experienced by children and not simply described to them.

Likewise the love and concern of God for his children is expressed to each child through the church school teacher. How he meets the shy child, the rebellious child, the withdrawn child, the hostile child will be an eloquent illustration of his faith. The attitude of the teacher is the method which underlies all external methods.

Briefly, it may be said that the physical surroundings and the emotional climate of a class are important factors in the use of methods. They become methods insofar as they can be planned areas in teaching. However, they are also subjects for inquiry in themselves, too broad to fit the scope of this book. They have been mentioned here so that the teacher, in exploring methods and planning their use, will be aware that the impact of a specific method will depend in part on these physical and emotional factors.

From now on the use of the word "method" in this book will refer more specifically to "techniques" which are aids to learning. This is what the teacher means in deciding between telling a story or reading from a book; using flat pictures or showing a filmstrip.

## Steps in Methodology

How does a teacher decide what method he will use or when he will use it? One factor which is familiar to those who know the nature of the small child is his need for variation, so a quiet activity is alternated with an active one. A story is followed by dramatization, or conversation by a game. Another consideration is the activity level of the children. When they first arrive they are alert and eager. This is when teachers use the methods requiring absorbed attention: listening to a story, discussion, or research. Toward the end of the session the children are tired, they are beginning to think of the next meal, and younger children may be getting restless. This is the time for activities which each child can take at his own pace.

Methods should also be selected according to an awareness of how a child learns the Christian faith in order that he may be strengthened in his growth as a child of God within the church. When a child enters the church school class he observes what is going on. Sooner or later he is drawn into its activities in terms of the specific methods being used. He becomes involved; he is a participant. Some even speak of his identifying with the character in a story, or the role he takes in dramatic play, or the things he sees in a picture, or the affirmations he makes in a hymn.

This involvement brings him to a place where he sees the

questions being asked and the decisions being called for. This is particularly noticeable in biblical stories. Simon has to decide to leave his fishing; Esau has to decide how to treat his returning brother. Or a contemporary story may bring the learner into a situation which he faces in daily life, but which he has not really evaluated. Decision is not a once-and-for-all matter to the Christian; it is something he faces daily as he seeks to be obedient to his Lord. So the opportunity for decision must be built into the methods which help the child to become involved in the events of the Bible, the church's history, or the life of the Christian in today's world.

This can result in deepening understandings about God and his purposes and growing awareness of what it means to be faithful to Christ. He responds with changing attitudes, and seeks to express these in many ways.

Teachers who try to follow these steps in choosing methods will find that the expressive work which the children do will show more originality and more care. Too often we have been guilty of asking them to express something which they have not really understood and to which, therefore, they were not ready to respond. It will be found that they can try to express feelings at home or obey rules at school more faithfully when they understand why they are asked to do this and when it is their response of personal decision. Their Christian faith is beginning to emerge from the category of secondhand experience (believing because of what the people we love tell us) to firsthand experience (believing because we have known God to act in our lives).

All this does not happen in one week, or in one year. But it can begin to happen in that time. Every teacher can know a deep sense of privilege as he reviews a year's work in terms of the development of each individual child in the class. Every year marks an important step in each pupil's development.

Just as these steps spread across the years, throughout the broad scope of the curriculum, so each of them may be found within a unit. The first week or so might see the use only of methods of participation with perhaps some beginning exploration of the decisions to be made; the last week or more of the unit may be built entirely around methods of communication: activities or plans of action.

## The Purposes of Methodology

What precisely are the objectives which a teacher has in mind in choosing a method? Most of the children in his class will probably already be members of the church. He will want to give them the week-by-week opportunity of participating in the presentation of God's historic actions as they are made known in biblical events and in the history of the church. The child needs to feel himself involved in these events as if he were living them as, in a sense, he is, for they are a part of his own past. This will help him to understand the biblical point of view. It can also help him to see how his situations, needs, and feelings often parallel those of the people in the biblical narrative. This gives him a broader perspective on immediate experience. The concerns of everyday life—putting up with younger brothers, keeping friends, getting along in school, obeying parents—may be difficulties for him but they certainly are not new or unique. Others have faced these, too, with varying responses, and the outcome was often influential in their ongoing experience. He can begin to understand the roots of his concerns as he sees why others have acted in certain ways: Joseph and his brothers in their jealousy; the kings of Israel in their differing responses to the words of the prophets; the Christians of the first three centuries facing persecution; the Reformers with their assurance that God had called them to revive his church.

This leads the child to see that life involves a series of decisions to be faced. There are the everyday decisions of what to do under specific circumstances. These, added up, make an approach to life and even a way of living. There are also the broader decisions with more ongoing results: to be friends with or reject a new child in the neighborhood; as a member of a group, to engage in constructive or destructive activities; to continue at church school or to drop out.

The Christian child, involved in the biblical and historical events of his faith, should be able to see all his decisions as his response to God.

In a recording of a conversation with children concerning their ideas of God, an adult moderator asks "When do you think about God?" Several of the children never had thought of him, had rejected the idea, or were indifferent. But those who responded said, "When I am in trouble" or "When everything goes wrong."* They knew that they needed help, and so were ready to receive it. The methods used in the church school should so involve the child in the deeper understandings of existence that he is able to receive the enabling gift of the Holy Spirit into his life.

Other specific methods have the further purpose of helping the child fulfill God's purposes for him in relation to per-

* Helen Parkhurst, *A Child's Ideas of God* (Alpark recording).

sonal and social situations, and to witness to his faith in various ways. Increased knowledge, deepened understandings, and changed attitudes should be accompanied by ways of acting that reflect a committed Christianity. These will include the ability to witness to one's faith in words, explaining Christian meanings as conversations arise among one's peers. Children do discuss religion, and sometimes the subject comes up in school under literature or social studies. They meet new children who come into a neighborhood. If they have developed a sense of concern as younger members of the church they will want to invite these others to come on Sunday morning without needing the encouragement of points in a contest or checkmarks toward an award.

These methods for helping the pupil fulfill God's purpose for him should enable him to understand what it means to act as a Christian in everyday life and give him the impetus to try, with God's help, to do so. No one will try to say that this is always easy, but only that those who love and serve Christ cannot do otherwise. There must also be the recognition that human beings are never perfect, that they will fail, but that God will make it possible for them continually to begin anew.

Another purpose pertains to the child who comes into the church school from a nonchurch or indifferent family background. To be sure, the parent has cared enough to send the child, and this is important. But such parents today often represent a generation who themselves were sent to church school by indifferent parents and who may have attended spasmodically. These children come to a church school class with no background of accumulated Christian teachings and experience to which the teacher can appeal. There is a primary need to help such children be drawn into an understanding of what the fellowship of the church is and to know themselves as welcome to enter alone. In a sense, the teacher becomes a sponsor, a substitute parent, and a primary influence. Since these children may first appear as mere observers, there will be a special need to draw them into the class group so that they will be open to its influences and willingly participate in its work as a group sharing in the Christian fellowship.

## Methods and Planning

So much for the "why" of methods. Teachers are more interested in getting into the practical aspects of the "how." The remainder of the book is concerned with this area. As you look at the variety of methods available you may well ask: "Which ones shall I choose?" "My session plans call for some methods and not others—can I try out some which interest me here?" "I am overwhelmed by the number of possibilities. Why don't we just stick to telling the story and asking questions about it?"

The specific discussion of methods which follows can help in using a method as well as indicating the varieties of activity available within a method. Suppose, for example, that your teacher's guide suggests a discussion about working together. The chapter on "Studying and Thinking" will help you, as you think of your own class, to understand why this is indicated. It will help you in guiding a discussion and suggest to you its possible results.

This discussion will further help you by indicating ways in which an experienced teacher, with an unusually alert class, can expand and modify methods to fit their own needs.

A session outline, even when fully written out, is still

meant to be only a guide to the teacher, rather than a necessary formula. Enriching an outline is an achievement of the perceptive and imaginative teacher and this is the only way in which an outline can be used satisfactorily within the many individual classes to be found in churches all over the country.

A few cautions will help the teacher to increase in skill in the choice of methods. To begin with, while variety is needed within one session, not all methods used should relate to the use of the same sense (seeing, or hearing, or touching). Seeing is a method. But if you were to begin a session with some selected flat pictures, go on to a filmstrip, and end with a discussion of a map—all in an effort to indicate to a class the setting for the Exodus—there would be a monotony in method. While each is a specific method, all belong to the same type. It would be better to establish the setting by the use of a biblical story (how the Israelites were desperate for food, or water, or meat), indicate the setting with pictures or filmstrip or map, discuss the situation of their need and how God met it, and close with some work or manual methods through which the child can disclose what he has learned.

Timing is an important part of any session. Sensitivity to the need to change the activity is something that grows with one's experience as a teacher. Partly this is a matter of having more ideas than can be used in any one session. It is also a matter of knowing the attention span of the group and their attention level at each given time during the session. Many teachers find that children, having had physical activity simply in getting from home to class, are able to settle down for their best period of thoughtful activity at the beginning of the session. This is the time for stories, research, and discussion. Then the teacher must be alert to realize, before the boys and girls get restless, that it is time to turn to another method. The children should be somewhat reluctant to turn aside, rather than being relieved to be finished. Now they need action. Just standing up and moving to another location in the room will do it. The introduction of a visual aid (map, picture, chalkboard) when they have been simply listening will be a change. Learning something in unison, such as a chance to use their voices in a hymn or Scripture passage, will be an activity. Various forms of dramatization are a possibility. Last, the children need some relaxed informality while working with individual freedom on a project.

Several points have been taken into consideration in the planning of such an outline (notice this in the outlines in your teacher's guide). There is variety of method. Each method is placed at the point at which the physical and mental resources of the child call for that particular type of method. The length of time spent on each method is gauged as a response to the attention and energy span of the children. There is a change of pace in the methods from quiet to active; from intensity of effort to relaxation in activities.

These make up some of the criteria for selecting appropriate methods. One may not attach an absolute "excellent" to any one method. The value of a method must always be weighed in relation to the teacher, the class, and the purposes of the unit of study. Storytelling is an excellent method, but if a teacher gets frightened at the thought of trying to tell a story, it would be better to learn how to read a story well, pausing to show pictures to the class and to stimulate their response to the written word. Making a notebook is an excellent way of learning, but if a class spent all last year making a notebook, this year's teacher would be wise to use another method of recording knowledge.

These are practical questions when one chooses what specific methods to use: Will my class be able to respond to it? Do I, the teacher, feel confident of my ability to use it? Does it further the objectives of the unit? Do we have the necessary equipment? Do we have the time?

The methods that follow can spark your imagination, increase your skill, and bring alive the session plans in your teacher's guide.

# 2. The Oldest Method:
## The Spoken Word

THE oldest method of teaching is that of storytelling. The biblical narratives which mean so much to us were remembered and retold orally for generations before being put into writing. Much of the Old Testament material, like the stories of the patriarchs, was retold to each generation and not written down until records began to be collected in the time of King David, about 1000 B.C. The New Testament remembrances of Jesus were preserved through the apostles, who told the story in order to convert their hearers. As they grew old, and the persecutions began, the people in the churches knew that it was time to commit these memories to writing in order that future generations might know the events and teachings in the life of their Lord.

Every church school teacher, when he tells a story, is in the line of a long and noble tradition which goes back to the apostles and beyond them to the singers of ancient Israel. He, too, is responsible for transmitting this heritage to a younger generation, and for telling the story accurately. If it is to him an exciting recital of his history, then he will be able to awaken his hearers to loyalty and devotion.

This is a story in which the storyteller himself is involved. These are his people; he belongs to the church. His hearers are also involved, the boys and girls to whom he tells the story. It is their history, also. They need to know themselves to be an ongoing part of it. Through it they learn what God has done for his people: how he chose them, led them, judged them, restored them, and in all things was more faithful to them than they to him. This assures them that God will be as faithful to his people today as he has always been in the past.

Teachers should think of biblical storytelling in this way. Never should they insert a story mechanically. Otherwise they will tell the substance of the material, but lose the excitement and significance of the event.

The wise teacher is prepared for storytelling. First he reads the narrative as he finds it in his teacher's guide or in the pupil's book. Then he always goes to the source itself, and reads the story from the Bible. This helps him see what changes may have been made in the retelling of the story. The curriculum writer of biblical stories sometimes feels he has good reason to make small changes from the original. He may wish to simplify the details for young children, or he may wish to add descriptive material which lengthens the narrative and makes it more vivid. This is legitimate insofar as it does not distort the biblical version. The teacher should know the original even though he may read the version in his curriculum material.

The skillful storyteller can absorb the biblical story and retell it in his own words. This enables him to use biblical phrases where he wishes and to elaborate on details when that seems indicated. Sometimes one can find a biblical narrative retold in a storybook in a style which gives pleasure to the reader as well as the hearer. The newer books are often attractively illustrated. The teacher may want to read the story verbatim, pausing to share the illustrations with the children.

## Pointers on Storytelling

A child must be able to follow a story in such a way that he becomes identified with one of the characters. This should be a character through whom he sees his own life and concerns in such a way as to know how God meets him and helps him in this situation. It follows, then, that a story will not be told from a point of view that permits the child to identify himself with Jesus. Rather, he should identify with the one who comes to Jesus and finds help. There are parallels in the life-situation story. The child needs to identify with a character who thinks and feels as he does in order that he may consider possible solutions and understand whether or not an ending is really satisfactory.

This raises the question of the hero story and the child's participation within its characterization. At this point the biblical hero is a helpful illustration. He is not perfect. He succeeds only insofar as he is faithful to God and is trying to fulfill God's purposes. This is perhaps a basic difference between the biblical hero and the secular hero figure. The former does not triumph by his own strength. When you choose a story, therefore, look carefully at the main figure and ask yourself with what kind of a person the children will be identifying. Will this help them to understand what it means to be a child of God?

Another point in storytelling is to begin with a well-written story. It is quite useless to try to use anything else, for the storytelling will fall flat and the children will quickly lose interest. A well-written story is vivid. It is a story which you, an adult, will want to read through to the end. It is a story which you can read many times and still enjoy. Every mother quickly learns to be grateful for the children's classics. They bring reading pleasure to both children and adults through endless bedtime repetitions. There are not too many well-written stories for church school use, but the teacher will be well rewarded for the time spent in ferreting them out. Such a story tells events vividly; one awaits developments with eagerness. The characters are so alive that one can picture them.

A well-written story will paint the setting with brief deft strokes that remain with the listener. The story will come to a satisfying climax and a brief ending. It does not need to be a happy ending in the popular meaning of that word. The Christian's happiness lies in being faithful to his Lord.

A fifth-grade class was reading a story about a young boy who lived in the time of one of the Roman persecutions. At the end of the story the boy's father was condemned to death. Several children in the class reacted negatively to the story. "I don't like it; it isn't a happy ending" said one. The teacher had the task of helping these children, imbued with a stereotype of the happy ending, to understand the more important criteria for evaluating the ending to a story: Is this inevitable in the development of the story? Have these people acted consistently within their characterizations? Were they loyal to themselves, to their friends, to God?

A well-written story will include dialogue. This will serve to distinguish one character from another as well as to forward action. Writing dialogue is an art. It involves varying the style to fit the characters as they speak. When dialogue is well-written, it is so good that the storyteller prefers to memorize or read rather than spoil the effect by putting the conversation in his own words. Dialogue makes a situation live. The hearers become involved in the action. They feel that they are speaking the words, or that they are being addressed. They somehow get inside the action and can feel what is happening.

A well-written (and well-told) story has a certain amount of literary style. The words are carefully chosen to convey exact meanings. They have color and emphasis. There is a rhythm which the storyteller can feel and convey by the rise and fall of his voice and the pace of his speaking. A skilled storyteller can take a not-too-well-written story, use the situation, and retell it in words that give it style and vivid characterization.

Similarly, the storyteller, by his manner of telling, will evoke a mood, convey the style, and express the rhythm intended. He will do this by the way in which he uses his voice, varying the range so that each character has a different inflection, and indicating changes in mood or setting by a rising or falling intonation. His face conveys the emotions which the story describes. He uses gestures to further the action. He is sensitive to timing, sometimes speaking slowly, at other times deliberately quickening the pace. He is not afraid of silence, but rather knows the effectiveness of a pause during which his hearers strain eagerly to know what significant word or action will follow. Of course, this kind of storytelling takes practice. It is a skill to be developed. But anyone who truly enjoys reading stories and appreciates literature can do it. There is no surer method of holding the attention of the class, involving them in a situation, and stimulating them to thought and action.

A good story does not moralize. By that we mean that it does not spell out the meaning at the end. The meaning will disclose itself as the story develops. The listener will come to the end of the story knowing what it means and what it is saying for him in his life. This is why story-writing and its telling is an art. Yet a surprising number of teachers, coming to the end of a story and finding no neat, moral ending, will spoil the writer's intent by adding a conclusion of their own, saying, "And so you can see that if we really want to show our love to God we will be kind to other people, even if they want to hurt us." This ruins a story, destroying the emotional and intellectual involvement which had already been established with the hearer. Some moralizers insert their points in the middle of the story. "Martha was a good girl, so she replied . . ." If Martha is a "good" girl, this will be apparent in her words and actions. Resist all temptation to spoil a story by such obvious additions!

The question arises as to whether the children should be

permitted to interrupt a story. If a teller is to preserve the mood, should not the hearers do the same? For the most part, this is true. No child should be permitted to interrupt in such a way as to break the mood for the rest. He should not interject some train of thought which it suggests to him, disturb another child, or try to tell the story himself. But it sometimes happens that a child is so caught up in the story that spontaneously he asks a question or speculates on the next step. With such an interruption, the teacher gently and tactfully incorporates the child's contribution into the fabric of the story. "Do you hope that this is what will happen? Let us see what Linda does next." Many are capable of becoming emotionally involved in a silent way. To evoke this involvement is part of the joy of storytelling.

There are many types of stories suitable for the purposes of Christian nurture. The teacher's guide may have a basic story for the session. Teachers will also want to use a story in a pre-session period, or on a day when the session plans move too quickly, leaving time at the end, or for some special situation as it arises. The biblical story is an obvious choice for many teachers. The curriculum, however, also includes the whole area of the later history of the church. This, too, is a part of our remembered past, and children should know that it is their responsibility to witness for the faith as others have done through many centuries. It is because of such fearless testimony that the church has been able to continue, in spite of disasters, to do the work God has given it to do. Stories from contemporary life can be used, if not always as examples of faith, then as illustrations of the need for Christian witness. Sometimes people of no faith show more sense of responsibility toward situations of need than do those who are nominally Christian. A story from such a situation might have much to say to sixth-graders as they begin to look toward confirmation and its meaning.

A vast range of story material is to be found in stories from the church in many parts of the world. Particularly exciting story material can be gathered today from newspapers and magazines, for Christianity is in the forefront of events in the emerging nations. Such stories help the child to realize that how Christians act, and the decisions which the church makes, are important. Children have been known to share their up-to-the-minute insights from church school in their social studies classes at school. This gives alert boys and girls the realization that the Christian faith is significant in today's world.

Persons are always important in story material. Some of the most vivid stories emerge from biographical material, either in the form of incidents or in pen portraits of lives. Whenever Christians are seen in action within the surrounding culture of their world, the boys and girls, conversant as they are with events from their everyday school life, become aware that their faith cannot be lived in a vacuum. They begin to perceive that what happens on Sunday morning is an integral part of and preparation for the life lived during the rest of the week.

Another source of material for storytelling is to be found in the immediate concerns of the children. This is a type of story which is sometimes contrived in plot and stilted in development. The storyteller, especially with an eye to church school use, tries to present ideal situations and very good children. The little girl helps at home; the boy resists the opportunity to cheat at school. Such stories leave the real, live, listening children cold. They know that this bears no resemblance whatever to their own lives. There, temptation is real and more often yielded to than overcome. They need to identify with story children who feel the conflict which they feel, who have bad thoughts and uncomfortable emotions, who sometimes win a victory, but often fail in their efforts to do what is expected. Children also face the puzzling situation of being rewarded when they do the right thing for the wrong reasons; and of being blamed when, with good intentions, they do something which their elders consider wrong. These are the vital areas for story situations which are life-centered. They give the teacher and class an opportunity later to talk about how God meets people in the midst of their concerns and how he guides them in the making of decisions. Sometimes the children themselves are the best source for story material. Sometimes a provocative picture from a newspaper or news magazine will suggest a story situation. The humorous cover of a magazine, or even a cartoon, may suggest the story which led up to the climax captured by the artist.

There are also stories from the natural world. By this we do not mean those in which animals appear to act as humans would. Some of these are a travesty on animal life. Others, however, indicate how animals, too, share the need for parental care, the search for shelter, the need for protection from the elements, the need to adapt to their surroundings, the joy in sunshine or in returning spring. Stories which revolve around the world of plants, the sea, or the vastness of the heavens lack vividness unless these are seen in relation to human beings who become aware of the providential goodness of God or the wonder of his creative work through interactions in his world.

The subject matter for stories is broad. Each type of

story has a function that cannot be as well met by another type. The purpose of any particular type is to help the child to identify himself in relation to God's redeeming love and purpose for his life.

## Varieties in Stories

While teachers tend to look upon biblical stories as basic for their teaching, it would be a mistake to overlook the riches of story material from other areas. An historical incident helps the child to realize the continuity of the Christian witness. There were not jumps in time from the first century to the sixteenth or to the twentieth. To be sure, the Bible is a unique witness to God's revelation, but the work of the Holy Spirit as continued in the life of the church is a fact which children should know. Until recently, there has been very little extra story material in this area to help teachers, but a few books have begun to appear. Your own curriculum will give you basic material. The historical story gives the child an opportunity to put himself into the picture with those who had to stand up for their faith, often under difficult circumstances. He learns that the church has been in India since the third century, in China since the fifth century, and in Japan since the fifteenth century. He begins to realize that the churches in the U. S. A. and Canada are younger churches.

The heroes of the faith were human, too. Sometimes their deeds were distorted by sin, and their purposes, seen in perspective, seem inclined more toward human desires than divine concern. In their greatest moments, they were certain of their calling, and they dared to speak for God at the risk of their lives. The memory of these people lives primarily through the life of the church. There is little way for children to hear these stories outside of church schools and Christian homes. They are part of our Christian family history.

The child is given the opportunity also of seeing how to view life as a Christian. If we confine ourselves to biblical figures, we leave the young learner in a puzzling situation. The Christian faith is placed in a distant time. The only biblical people to face the world as Christians were those reported in the Acts of the Apostles. The problems of being a Christian in the twentieth-century culture can be found only in more recent historical material and in contemporary reports.

Stories of historical people and events should open up the possibility of betrayal as well as of witness, of faithlessness as well as faithfulness. They can present the further problem of how to treat those who are faithless. This was a concern during the third-century persecutions. It was a concern during the Reformation and became a problem again during the 1940's (and still is in communist countries). If a person betrays his faith because of fear, or even a sense of family responsibility, and later wishes to come back into the Christian community, can he be received with understanding? Can the pupils accept the possibility that some are not as strong as others?

A note is in order here concerning a kind of story, which has been favored at times, in which people who were outstanding in their humanitarian work became prototypes of what Christians ought to be. These are fine stories which will usually find a place in the school curriculum. The question to ask about stories concerning both historical and contemporary personages is in reference to the motivation for action. When this has come from a sense of calling, as obedience to God's purpose, and as an expression of the life of the baptized Christian in the world, then it is one through which the child can see what it means to be a Christian. He is helped to see that the purposes of God for the church are fulfilled in the lives of God's people in the world. This is not a general "love thy neighbor" impulse, but rather being Christ to the neighbor.

The experience-centered contemporary story is another area through which to enrich teaching. People are always interested in what depicts lives like their own. It is this kind of novel or short story that most people read, either in popular books or in the current magazines. They know how it feels to identify with a character whose life resembles their own. It gives them momentary escape, helps them to see the solution of a problem, or assures them that their life is not so difficult as it appears to be in some moments.

By the same token, children also need stories from life situations, so that they can see their concerns through a story character with whom they can identify. Any teacher knows something of the children's areas of concern. Some are the same in Grade 6 as in Grade 1, while others are more evident in particular years. There are family concerns such as getting along with brothers and sisters, accepting the new baby, being understood by mother, moving to a new home, or living up to expected standards. There are school concerns, such as liking a strict teacher, meeting work demands, trying to achieve in sports, getting good grades, becoming popular. These are essentially questions of relationships which involve ethical problems. The child is asking: "Does the Christian faith have anything to say to me in these situations? Can God help me in these daily needs?"

Every child has certain basic needs (principally arising from the need to be loved), and there are a number of ways in which he needs to grow. His anxieties, and much of his unhappiness, with the resultant behavior, arise through his misunderstandings and frustrations as he seeks fulfillment of these needs and the accomplishment of these tasks. A story which lifts up an area of concern in a realistic way helps him to see himself and to consider how to act. The word "realistic" needs to be emphasized here. Far too much church school material has been extremely unrealistic. It has presented a "typical" situation with an "ideal" solution. This is disastrous. It convinces the child that the church is not aware of the difficulties in the way of a solution. It particularly ignores the emotional aspects of life. The children listen politely and give the expected answers. They are convinced that the church knows nothing about real life and that the Christian faith could not possibly be able to help them.

Real stories are not always pleasant. They tell about the little girl who, being asked to set the table, replies "Must I?" and continues talking on the telephone with a friend. Or the boy who does everything he is told to do in school, but is burning up inside with a feeling of being unfairly treated.

In using true-to-life stories, if there is real confidence between teacher and children, the boys and girls will respond to such situations, admitting that they sometimes feel this way. They will give you more real story material than you can ever use. They will help one another by sharing ways in which they have been able to understand these adults and live within the necessary framework of life.

Here is the place for turning to the Bible and finding out

the good news for boys and girls. Only when they recognize their troubles are they able to hear the biblical word speaking to their lives. Now God's assurance that he is near them, that he helps, forgives, and restores can become a living word. These concerns now become religious issues, for it can be more readily seen that the only deep solution is in religious terms.

What goes on during a church school session can be pertinent to the rest of the week. Thus they learn through vicarious experience, and can begin to think of their everyday lives as a witness to the faith they celebrate. At this point we might remember that early liturgies used to end with a dismissal, a sending forth into the world: "Go forth in peace." A church school class needs to do exactly that.

Other experience-centered stories revolve around the child's understanding of man's place in the natural world. He feels himself much a part of the space age and his thoughts are set in distant planets. Contrary to past church school situations, the present child wonders less about the beauty of the world than its destructiveness. How do we understand God's purposes in floods, earthquakes, forest fires, bombs, he will ask. Stories must help the child to deal with these real problems, to understand man's use and misuse of the planet of which he is steward. It must help him to accept the basic facts of the natural world, such as splits in the earth which cause earthquakes, as part of God's creation. To grasp the difference between this kind of disaster and that evil which proceeds from the free will of man is a part of learning. His questions about death are implicit in the questions about disaster, and he needs to know the Christian's assurance of eternal life. Story material can raise the problems. Biblical words can give understandings in terms of the creative, providential, and redemptive work of God.

Boys and girls rarely learn to live with wars and rumors of wars. They need stories which help them to see what happens. They need to be able to acknowledge their fears. They can, in the church, understand the meaning of judgment and of redemption. Older children may well ponder Jesus' parables of judgment and see the parallels of the destruction in the first century and the threats of our own century. Only the church school teacher can give these children an assurance that contains more hope than a bomb shelter.

## Varieties in Storytelling

*The Open-Ended Story.* Everyone knows the classical form of a story: opening, development, climax, close. The open-ended story is a variation of this. It is a story which revolves around a problem or concern. It develops the characters vividly in order that the listeners may identify with them. But the open-ended story stops just before the climax; the solution is not given. The listener is left with the question: What happened next? Here is the listener's chance to answer what he would do, or how he feels, or what "should" happen. The teacher who uses this type of story must be willing to accept suggested endings from his pupils which do not fit into any ideal pattern. Their endings will reveal much about the thinking of the boys and girls in the class. Children are perceptive in knowing the probable solution as over against the "correct" answer.

A teacher might use the open-ended story form with stories already in the teaching materials, stopping short before the ending and saying, "Let's put your ending on the story." The teacher may be surprised at their endings. If one stops to think about it, any brief incident clipped from a newspaper or magazine may provoke a good open-ended story. The description of a humorous situation from a cartoon might become the beginning of a story.

*The Illustrated Story—Flannelgraph.* There is a real place for both the unillustrated story in which the children can exercise their own imaginations in visualizing the characters and the action, and the story supported by illustration. One form of illustrated story is the flannelgraph. This consists of the use of figures which have an abrasive or sticky material (sandpaper or flannel) on the back. This enables them to adhere to a piece of board fronted with flannel. Such boards may be bought or can be inexpensively constructed. Cut-out books will sometimes supply usable figures, if the teacher prefers not to buy them. As each character in the story is introduced, he is put on the board. He can be moved about in the course of the action. A story, to be effectively told with the flannelgraph, needs to be restructured in terms of the medium itself. One needs first to establish the setting, then introduce each character individually and descriptively. A story almost needs to be told in scenes, like a play. Flannelgraph holds the attention of the listeners. However, it can lose its spell if used too often. It is wise to confine its use to one or two grades; otherwise, it soon becomes "old stuff" to the children.

*Chalkboard.* Some teachers find the chalkboard an aid to storytelling. Chalkboard technique is similar to that of flannelgraph, except that the teacher sets the stage with figures on the board. Admittedly, this could take skill, but any teacher will find that stick figures are easily drawn and focus attention without requiring perfection. They also allow the pupil's imagination to play.

*Puppets.* Puppets of various sorts can be used in initial storytelling, although they are more often used for the retelling of a story in dramatic form. (Retelling will be considered in the next chapter.) A teacher may use two hand puppets, turning to them as she repeats dialogue passages, addressing the class for descriptive and narrative parts of the story. In this situation, the puppets are being used much as the flannel figures on the board.

*Reading Books.* The use of outside reading books should also be mentioned under storytelling. These are an invaluable resource for teachers who want to make the most of every minute. A small collection can be built up not too expensively and will be useful to many teachers for a number of years, since children like to hear a good story retold. Primary reading books can often be read in short periods of time. A book for older children usually will be read through a chapter at a time.

The alert teacher who reaches the classroom early gathers the firstcomers around for a story unless the teacher's guide suggests a different activity. The story may be picked up again and read to children near the end of the session if they are completing activity work at this time. This is helpful to the ones who finish quickly; it also relaxes the painstaking worker who can go at his own pace and not feel that everyone is waiting for him. Parents arrive at the end of the session to find serene absorption. This is enrichment material a teacher should not neglect. Those who have a fairly long class session may be able to plan for such reading each week. Use the text as written; do not try to retell it unless you are pressed for time and need to condense a section. Be sure to pause if the children have comments or questions, for reading a book does not require the same concentration that telling a brief story does. Turn the book toward them and let them share the pictures as you read along.

Teachers often have questions as to how to use the pupil's reader meaningfully. The most important point to remember is that the writers have worked to make these good stories. Since stories are meant first of all to be enjoyed, let the children enjoy them. Give the children some background, letting them read silently until they have finished a story. Then bring in thoughtful questions about the meaning. Avoid questions like "Who was John?" or "What did Peter do next . . .?" Rather, ask "Did John do the best thing? Why did Peter feel that way?" The whole impact of a story comes in the first reading; take care how it is done.

The second time around is different. In considering any related questions, you may wish to backtrack. Then you might ask a particular child to read a paragraph. You might ask two or three to assume roles and read dialogue. But choose the readers carefully. Give the good readers the long words, or the difficult passage; the hesitant readers, a simple line. In this way each can use the skills he has and no one becomes either impatient or embarrassed.

Whatever form the story takes, it is undoubtedly the backbone of many teaching sessions, for the story is at home in many settings and can be used with classes of all sizes.

# 3. Drama: Words in Action

THE Bible has been referred to as "the drama of redemption." The phrase is used to highlight the fact that the Bible is a book of action. God does not merely speak; his purposes are made known through the events of national history and in the lives of people.

Some of the material in the Bible seems to be specifically dramatic in form. The Book of Job consists of an opening narrative followed by a series of addresses by Job, his three friends, and the voice of God. One can see the book as a dramatic recital in which the participants try to understand the meaning of suffering and the nature of divine retribution. The Song of Songs is also drama. Indeed one version of the Bible arranges the material in dramatic form as a series of love songs between a bride and groom, and uses a chorus at one point. There are no narrative portions.*

Some of the psalms are dramatic in form. They were written to be used for religious festivals or liturgical events. One can hear the words of the priests alternating with the words of the choir. Sometimes there are responses by the people. Some suggest motion, a processional or a return. Indeed, all liturgy involves dramatic action where the words, both sung and spoken, are accompanied by motions. Activity in the pattern of corporate worship has always been a part of the Christian tradition.

*Dramatic Reading.* Drama is a representation of events through direct address. Whereas a story describes the setting and delineates a character in words, drama uses other methods of establishing this background. The way the characters look and act, the tone of voice, and the manner of speaking establish the kind of persons they are. No one will describe this to the listeners. Sometimes the very way the characters act suggests the setting. Everyone has at some time seen a great actor who could create a role with no setting, no props, and only a stylized use of costume. This is the art of the monologuist, and we do well to remember this in the church school use of drama. The elaborate is not essential.

The biblical narratives themselves may be used as dramatic reading—even those which were not drama in their

* Richard G. Moulton (ed.), *The Modern Readers' Bible* (New York: Macmillan, 1930).

original form. It is surprising how much direct discourse there is in the Gospels if one reads them with this in mind. Some of the parables include conversation. Some of the Old Testament narratives have dialogue. Whole passages from the prophets are addresses. The Gospel of Mark, without much difficulty, could be arranged for dramatic reading. With one person in the role of narrator, others would take the roles as they appear. As early as the sixth grade, such material could be used by the pupils, and not simply read by the teacher.

*Choral Reading.* Choral reading is another dramatic form to which the Bible lends itself. This has the practical value of being usable with a large group as well as a small one, and of involving all the children. Light voices balance heavy ones, while solo voices stand out to enunciate the words of a speaker. This technique may be used with the psalms. It may also be used for narratives, with the chorus becoming the narrator. Even second and third grade children, beginning to read the psalms, can learn an appreciation of this literature and skill in reading it through the use of this technique. We adults sometimes forget, being so accustomed to the use of the responsive reading ourselves, that children have to learn how to read responsively—when to come in, how to keep in unison with the whole congregation, how to grasp the meaning while alternately reading aloud and silently.

## Forms of Dramatization

Drama serves several purposes. It may recreate events. This is historical drama, a way by which listeners or actors can become involved in history and see its live quality.

Though drama brings out the uniqueness in each historical happening or era, it also illustrates the constant recurrence of common human factors. A number of biblical plays do this: Andrew Obey's *Noah,* Marc Connelly's *Green Pastures* (which catches the whole sweep of the biblical story), Paddy Chayefsky's *Gideon,* Archibald MacLeish's *J.B.* (Job), Dorothy Sayers' *The Man Born to be King.* The medieval mystery play, a retelling of biblical episodes, does this in a less sophisticated way.

Do these illustrations seem appropriate only for adults? The teacher who enjoys literature will always want to explore the possibilities with the children. Fifth- and sixth-graders will be able to interpret some scenes. Indeed, they may find the twentieth-century biblical play *Green Pastures* more comprehensible than the seemingly simpler medieval biblical play. The closing scene of *Green Pastures,* in which God comprehends the meaning of suffering, might be a helpful introduction to the Passion season. The *Quem Quaeritis strophe,* the oldest fragment of drama in the English language, is readily available and can be used by the boys and girls at Easter. This is a chorus reading between the angel and the women before the empty tomb. "Whom seek ye, Christian women?" is the opening challenge. When we remember the developed reading skills of many fifth- and sixth-graders, the possibilities of using dramatic material of good literary style does not seem out of the way.

Again the teacher's guides and helps will indicate appropriate materials, but occasionally there may be opportunity for something extra. In any case, the teacher should be aware of the values of drama.

*Readers' Theater.* Reading dramatic material around a circle is not an inspiring activity, and full-scale production

44

is hardly a possibility. But there are forms of dramatic reading being developed in university drama departments which hold promise as methods for church school teaching. One of these is "readers' theater." In this technique, a story, episode, novel, narrative poem, or play is used. The narrative, or descriptive portion, is taken by one person; roles of specific characters are assumed by others. The readers stand or sit on high stools at reading desks on which the scripts are placed. The placing of the desks signifies the relation of the characters to one another. In this setting, addressing the audience rather than one another, the drama is enacted. The actual form is flexible. Sometimes all the players stand in a semicircle in the back of the "stage" area, while those participating in a scene come forward. The simplicity of the approach suggests that this would be a valuable teaching device with fifth- and sixth-graders who have both reading skills and dramatic interests.

Readers' theater is simple enough to give enjoyment to a class by itself or for the boys and girls to present at a home for senior citizens or a parents' meeting.

*Chamber Theater.* A more elaborate technique is contained in "chamber theater." This falls somewhere between readers' theater and a full-blown dramatic presentation. It is especially useful for putting story material into dramatic form. For this reason it may be suggested to the teachers of younger children. In this technique the material is acted out. The narrative portions are spoken by one person who may stand to the side, or who may hover around the edge of the action as if in the role of the author. Dialogue is both spoken and acted. Setting and props are not used, but some semblance of costuming (use of particular colors in dress, for example) may be attempted. This form suggests a way

45

of retelling biblical narratives, substituting, where necessary, direct address for indirect address. Examples are the Joseph story, Moses in Egypt, and conversations between Jesus and the disciples.*

These forms of drama employ the exact words of a written work. They should be used only where the literary quality of the written word is such that the words merit exact reading or even memorizing. Many of the plays written for children are poor in quality. The characters do not seem real; they merely mouth words. The setting is artificial, the plot contrived. Do not waste practice time on anything which does not have a good understanding of the biblical faith and a cogent expression in language and action.

*Creative Dramatics.* A more widely usable form of dramatics is that which is popularly known as creative dramatics. This is the evolution of a play from a story situation through action and dialogue developed by the children. It is not as spontaneous as it might seem. In fact, teachers who try the technique and fail do so because they have mistakenly thought it could be casually used. The emphasis in creative dramatics lies in the delineation of character and the working out of a problem situation.†

The theme could be historical, biblical or contemporary. Let us see how it works out using a biblical story, the story of Rehoboam and Jeroboam (1 Kings 12). The crucial part

* For a discussion of chamber theater see the article by Robert S. Breen under that heading in the *Westminster Dictionary of Christian Education,* edited by Kendig Brubaker Cully (Philadelphia: Westminster, 1963).

† See Winifred Ward's *Playmaking with Children.* (2d ed.; New York: Appleton-Century-Crofts, 1957) and her pamphlet, *Drama with and for Children,* U. S. Dept. of Health, Education, and Welfare, 1960.

of the narrative is the struggle for power, Rehoboam's choice of oppression and Jeroboam's choice of revolt. After the class has read the story, they would need to decide what parts they want to use, what scenes to choose, and what characters to have in each scene. Then they would concentrate on the first scene, after the death of Solomon. Will it be Jeroboam's reflecting on his exile and what he hopes to do? What kind of person is he? What would he say? Several children would take turns speaking as Jeroboam. The teacher would jot down the important points they would want to have in this soliloquy. Next the class might turn to Rehoboam, summoned to Shechem. Will he be discussing this with someone? How will the conversation go? Different members of the group would try out this scene. The climax of the play is the meeting at Shechem. There is room here for everyone. Teacher and pupils would plot the setting, the action, the characters, the conversation. Here is a Bible story which dramatically sets forth a choice which was faced by the Hebrew people, and a choice which, with other names and other phrases, is faced repeatedly by citizens of many nations. The advantage of this type of drama is that the children use their own wording, based on their understanding of the people and events. They feel an attachment for the characters and situation. They have been led to an analysis of history.

Creative dramatics can be done with children in third grade and up. Whether or not it would be a useful technique with younger children depends in part on the background of the children, whether they feel free to explore "let's pretend" situations, and the interest of the teacher. Each teacher has particular skills and will find the most satisfying results in using those in which he is best qualified.

*Role-play.* The role-play is similar to creative dramatics. It points to another purpose of drama, the playing out of a problem situation in order to understand the issues involved. The open-ended story may be role-played. After the story has been built up the class suggests the possible endings. Then members of the group may take roles and play out the story to its completion in those different ways suggested. This gives them the "feel" of the people in the problem situation more directly than they have had it through story and discussion. It will deepen the sense of reality in any discussion which comes after the role-play. In fact, there should always be a follow-up discussion in which the parts (not the acting or actors) are criticized by watchers and participants.

Role-play can also be used if only the outline of a problem is set up. If someone complains about a playtime situation, the teacher may say, "Let's look at this a moment. What's the situation? Who is involved? Let's act it out." Then, by imagining themselves in the situation, the boys and girls can see more clearly why the other people act as they do. Essentially, role-playing is a way of seeing the other person's point of view by putting ourselves in his place. It also helps us to see how others view us. This suggests a warning: a child should never be assigned a role in which he might feel hurt. If a child shows timidity, do not ask him to take the role of the child who is being taunted. If a child feels he has been wronged, do not ask him to take a role by which he will have to see suddenly and clearly in a class situation where his own fault lay. Role-playing must be used sympathetically. It clarifies, but it should not judge.

Nor is role-playing to be confused with more technical forms such as psychodrama or sociodrama. The former is used by specially trained persons to help people with emotional problems live through their experiences and come into new insights. The problems with which you will be dealing are the normal, everyday responses of boys and girls who find frustrations in living and loving. Sociodrama is used in order to analyze difficult social situations and to help people involved in such situations to see the forces operating against (and toward) solutions. Both of these forms of drama are used with young people and adults. Role-play can be handled in pantomime. This way it can be used even with primary children.

*Singing Games.* Games, especially singing games, are another form of dramatic play. These are more widely used with preschool children, but teachers of first grade and those engaged in the more relaxed activities of vacation school should not cut out their use too early. Such games are a link with the earlier grade. The old planting song, "Oats, peas, beans, and barley grow" might, indeed, have more meaning in the first grade than in the kindergarten, where it is more frequently used.

*Charades.* Charades are another form of pantomimic dramatic play. Biblical characters can be portrayed this way, or a biblical story, or even a word. Children at all ages like guessing games. Older groups like word study. A group in weekday or vacation school might learn by taking apart theological words and guessing them as they are pantomimed, one syllable at a time.

*Puppets.* There is a growing interest in puppets as a medium through which to express drama. The simplest form is a stick puppet. After the children have heard or read a story, each chooses a character and makes a paper figure, coloring it with paints or crayon. Or the pupil could paint a face on a small paper bag. The bag is put over a dowel stick about a foot long (available, cut to size, at any hardware store) and perhaps stuffed with tissue and tied in at the neck and waist with string. The children will need to make a waist-high stage behind which to work their puppets. Then the puppets will act on the top, the children who hold them being seated behind the screen. Or a really high curtain could be set up, behind which the children stand to operate the puppets over their heads. The use of puppets involves several auxiliary activities. First the puppets must be made. Then the story must be planned, remembering the limited locomotion of a stick puppet. The background stage needs to be made. Finally the production is put together. This involves a reasonable block of time, either during one or two sessions or continuously for a number of weeks. Simple as a stick puppet is, the child projects himself into this figure and will sometimes act with an abandon that he would not display were he doing the acting in person. This is an important point to remember. The technique has particular value for use with children who feel shy or awkward when asked to assume a role.

The hand puppet requires more work, but it also has greater versatility. It requires a skill which may not be found below third or fourth grade. It is hardly more than an elbow-length glove with three fingers. The center finger will need to be stuffed in some manner to be the head, the two side fingers form the hands. The rest of the glove covers the arm of the manipulator up to the elbow. The head could be of papier-mâché moulded around a paper ball. The head could be stuffed with rags or cotton. The face will need to be painted on, and hair could be painted or made of yarn. The dress which partially hides the arms of the figure and the arm of the manipulator will suggest what the puppet represents by material, color, and pattern. The completed figure can be fitted onto the thumb and first two fingers of the hand. The index finger goes into the head. With practice, one can convey various feelings and actions by turns of the head and action of the arms. Hand puppets are perhaps more useful for conversation than for action. The action projects the pupil's own feelings into this type of puppet better than onto the stick puppet, for the hand puppet becomes a veritable extension of the self. Like the other puppet, it may be used behind a screen and two puppets can sometimes engage in vigorous interaction, especially on the hands of small boys. Perhaps each child needs a hand puppet for an alter ego! Since types of hand puppets are produced commercially, many children will have had experience in their use and can help the teacher to understand how to work them.

Occasionally a puppet show has successfully conveyed a story to a television audience, but as a culture we have been much too unappreciative of the value of the puppet as a symbol which conveys truth by the very virtue of the fact that it seems unrealistic or nonfactual. True puppets or marionettes are far more complicated to make and to use. These would have to be a hobby of someone in the parish, and would find their best use in a year-round group which became so interested that it wanted to give some weekday time to the construction effort.

## Drama as a Teaching Method

What makes good drama? The characters must be authentic. They do not have to be everyday persons; indeed, they could be quite unusual. But they must be true to their own characterization; they must seem plausible to the reader or viewer. They must show humor as well as seriousness, and some goodness mixed with evil, for the human personality is always complex. If drama is to be a mirror put to life, it must reflect what can really be seen. Dramatic characterization shares this necessity with the characters in a story. The child character who is too good is false; the adult who always steers a straight and unwavering course is unreal. No one can have empathy with or learn from such a character.

The situation must be vivid. This refers not only to geographical or historical background, but to the immediate situation in which the characters find themselves. Unless the setting is quite frankly meant to be imaginative, it should definitely be plausible. Weak drama contains situations which are neither one nor the other. There needs to be a situation calling for real effort of thought, decision, and action. The contrived play is shown up as soon as real people start to discuss it. It seems too trival to waste time on and the group soon tears it apart.

The dialogue must be authentic. It must sound as if real people are speaking, using the language and sentence structure which characterizes the people involved. Good dialogue in a children's play is easy for the boys and girls to read, and even easy to memorize. It is their living language. The style and development of the play must have some literary quality. There is plenty of stuff in print that is not worth bothering with. On the other hand, it doesn't need to be Shakespeare to be good.

The production of drama in its most informal setting is an area in which the professional is very quickly separated from the amateur. The latter tries with painstaking thoroughness to recreate a biblical or historical situation. The former, with studied casualness, may use no setting but a backcurtain, and may depend for the effectiveness of costumes simply on suggestions of a style.

Many people, hearing the word "drama," picture a special stage, an elaborate stage design, realistic settings and costumes, and carefully studied action. Simplicity is the keynote in the theater today. The drama must be good enough so that the words shine through the action, and the power of the words evokes both the characters and the setting. Many workers in the experimental theater, either off-Broadway or in the university, consider a stage at the long end of the room, high up and separated by apron and proscenium, to be a barrier to communication. They use no curtain, and signal the beginning of the action by a change from darkness on the stage to light (with the dimming of the auditorium lights). They have steps down from the stage which bring the actors even into the middle of the audience, or in the center of the room, surrounded by the audience. Actors walk on instead of appearing through the usual stage door. Elaborate settings are replaced by simple curtains where color alone may suggest the mood of the upcoming scene. Some scenes are staged in front of a closed curtain. The three-act play is replaced by a series of episodes with an intermission pause at a significant point. The costumes suggest the period and character rather than trying to imitate it.

Many of the elements which the amateur might think essential to drama are really irrelevant. Of course, your church school class was not planning to produce full-scale drama anyway, so why elaborate on all this? The fact of the matter is that often more effort goes into elaborate costuming even in church schools than in the understanding of the words and theme. The weakness in the use of drama for teaching often lies in the fact that the meaning of words and purpose of action are lost in an overlay of props, settings, and costumes which form convenient ways of releasing children's energies. When we let ourselves be misled into encouraging this sort of thing, we have failed to be sensitive to the inborn gift of imagination and empathy which we should be encouraging the child to use.

Most efforts at religious drama, learned or spontaneous, will be done within the class, with everyone participating by turn, for mutual learning and insight. Occasionally, it may be decided that a story, scene, or episode should be prepared more thoughtfully and presented at some special event. There might even be an open house for parents at which the boys and girls present their work.

When a teacher first begins to use creative drama, asking individuals to assume roles and then proceed with speech and action, the result may be chaotic. He should not retreat in discouragement. He should simply call the group together and give them a chance to see what has happened. It will become evident that several first steps have not been taken seriously enough: plotting the scenes, developing one scene, describing the characters, and sketching in the dialogue orally. This has to be done by the whole group. Then children are chosen for specific roles in one scene. These are sent to a designated area of the room for playing the scene and the others are specifically directed to encourage them by listening and watching. When they know that all will eventually have a chance, they soon learn how to wait attentively. The second round will be a distinct improvement. The third trial will bring forth seriousness of purpose on the part of the players, who will by now be showing some emotional response to each other. They will have grasped the pattern. They will be ready to discuss the situation and the characters and to understand the problem involved.

The purpose of informal drama is to let the children see themselves in the same situation as that which faced a biblical or historical character, or the person in an experience-centered story. By seeing themselves thus they become able to understand the springs of action. They begin to know why an event happened as it did and not otherwise (human beings acted as they are and not as anyone would like to imagine them to be). They can begin to grasp both the need for God's redemptive activity and to see how the grace of God can work in the situation. Drama has begun to serve a religious purpose, not because the material was specifically that of a religious issue, and certainly not because someone thought up an "ideal" situation, but because participants and onlookers can learn to put themselves in the situations of others and see how God has worked in those lives, or else see their own situation worked out by author and actors who present problem and solution realistically and with Christian love.

## Drama Which Is Seen

The purpose of this chapter has been to show how boys and girls, by participating in dramatic action in its varied forms, can gain new insights and deeper religious awareness.

It has been suggested, however, that it is also possible to gain understanding by indirect participation. Just as the hearer participates by empathy in the story read or told to

55

him, so does the audience which watches a play. Children's drama has a place in the yearly calendar of many communities, and the church school teacher should be aware of the plays being offered. There may be one or more each year which will offer food for discussion in the church school. If most of the class attend the play as a school event, the teacher will draw on their experience when next the class meets. He can plan attendance at such a play with one or more parents assisting at the theater party.

Movies are drama when they tell a story, delineate character, evoke a mood, or present a situation. Television presents many situations which children are in the habit of watching. The teacher might well be aware of favorite programs, thinking about the religious implications (positive or negative).

Many plays have been put on records. This may be a more effective form of studying (particularly for ten-year-olds) than trying to read a section from a serious play. For many children it is easier to understand by hearing than by reading. Often biblical stories, in their transfer to records, are dramatized rather than retold.

Learning through hearing (stories) already has been discussed. This chapter has been primarily concerned with learning through action (drama). We turn next to the ways of learning through seeing.

# 4. Learning Through Seeing

We live in a picture civilization. Most civilizations have done much of their teaching through visual methods. The earliest known commentaries of men are the prehistoric cave drawings found in the South of France. The civilizations of the ancient world are known today through pictures, heiroglyphs, and artifacts. The way of life of the ancient Greeks and Romans can be reconstructed through the embellishments of their buildings. Many of these "things to

57

look at" were used for education as well as beauty. The glorious stained-glass windows of the Gothic cathedrals were used as teaching devices, as were the intricate carvings in niches and over archways.

Picture magazines hold millions of subscribers to whom the whole printed explanation says less than the impression made by the angle at which the photograph was taken. Slick magazines sell the housewife new products through better-than-real color illustrations. Children spend hours a day before the television screen. They line up before the movie box-office faithfully every Saturday afternoon. The supermarket products vie with one another for the shoppers' attention, each one with larger print, brighter color or more exotic packaging than the next. Adults, as well as children, do most of their learning by seeing.

### Identification Through Pictures

The child learns from pictures by becoming a witness to the events which the pictures describe. He feels part of the people or the events. He is captured by the mood which the pictures intend to evoke. Since biblical pictures are so much taken for granted in church school teaching, the teacher needs to look at each one carefully, asking the question, "With whom is the viewer supposed to identify in this picture?" In the discussion of stories, it was pointed out that in the biblical narrative the reader often identifies with the person who comes to Jesus in need and that biblical stories should be carefully oriented. The same criterion holds for pictures. If the picture is to convey the meaning of a gospel story, it must be so oriented that the boys and girls, with the people in the picture, look toward Jesus and his gospel.

This is nowhere better illustrated than it is in the famous Rembrandt etching, "Christ Preaching to the Poor." The scene is dominated by the figure of Christ, from whom light and warmth emanate. The gazes of all are upon him, but the expressions vary. Some figures stand in the background, resistant; others question; others turn eagerly toward him for healing. Those who look at the picture become a part of the figures who gaze upon him. With which type of viewer do they associate?

Church school art has not always remembered this necessity of careful association. Sometimes the composition has been such that the viewers identified with Jesus as he went about helping others. The deliberate point of view of such pictures was to encourage the child to be helpful, as Jesus was. However laudable the moral intention of such a picture may be, it is contrary to the biblical point of view, and therefore, as a picture, is a distortion of whatever biblical story it seeks to represent. In the Bible, the hearer should identify with those whom he resembles and not with the one to whom he looks for help. To identify with Jesus becomes an impossible change of role. It avoids the necessary insight whereby the viewer sees his need and becomes aware of what, by the grace of God, he may become.

Another point to remember in choosing biblical pictures is that truth and accuracy are important in relation to the events being portrayed and the emotions depicted, rather than to the physical background of the story. There was an effort, in church school pictures of the recent past, to try to achieve an accurate biblical background. Often, more time was spent on this kind of detail than on developing an understanding of the story or idea to be illustrated.

Classical artists depict the events as they seem to them

and the background becomes a part of the interpretation of the event. The landscape will resemble Italy, Holland or Germany, according to the dwelling-place of the artist. The dress, in cut and color, will suggest the person rather than the cultural situation. In this way artists are able to show the impact of the event, to reveal depth of character and to suggest the deeper levels of meaning. The Bible itself is not concerned with external things, but with the effects of the confrontation between God and man. The point is that the teacher using this kind of art should concentrate on the impact of the meaning, not on accuracy or wealth of detail.

A picture to be used with children needs to be checked against the biblical record to be sure that both are saying the same thing. Does the art share the biblical point of view or does it present the artist's private interpretation? For instance, Tintoretto's painting "The Conversion of St. Paul" is a distinctive approach to a biblical description. At a casual glance, this seems to be mostly a Renaissance painting: people in sixteenth century dress, Italian scenery, sleek horses rearing, dashing soldiers drawing swords. But when one studies the picture, several timeless points emerge: somehow the huddled figure of the apostle is in the center, and the blinding light is over all. The impression one gets is that of utter confusion, a confusion caused by the piercing light. The confusion of men and horses is simply the outer manifestation of the confusion in the whole being of Saul. One is reminded of the narrative in Acts 9: "Suddenly a light from heaven flashed about him. And he fell to the ground and heard a voice . . . The men who were traveling with him stood speechless" (*Acts 9:3, 4, 7*). There had to be action in a picture which sought to depict this event.

The artist need not be religious in the conventional sense

of the word, but he should have been gripped by the biblical story, and the gift for painting makes it possible for him to put the story on canvas. Through him, many who look at the original picture or at a good reproduction are confronted by the biblical message.

No matter what we may wish to enjoy personally, all who teach children have a responsibility for giving them only good art. Few people are art critics, but all can learn what makes some pictures good authentic art and others simply mediocre attempts at imitating reality. One should become familiar with good pictures—month after month—until he knows what a picture is supposed to do, even if he does not accept it with personal enjoyment. If he does not live near an art gallery, the public library should have a few books containing fine reproductions. A day will almost certainly come when he will look again at some of the pictures he used to like, and see their shallowness. The complexity of art, which used to be confusing, will have become interesting by familiarity. The enjoyment of a fine painting does not diminish, for there is always something new to be found in it.

## Pictures and the Life of the Child

Not all the pictures used in the church school need to be biblical. It is a useful plan to hang one fine reproduction in each classroom. A class whose course for the year was centered in the creative work of God saw in their room a framed reproduction of Van Gogh's "Starry Night." A class of small children looked each week at the warm relationship between a mother and her child expressed in Bernard Karfoil's print "Mother and Child" The intent enjoyment with which the little girl spoons the food from her bowl in Picasso's "The Gourmet" suggests Thanksgiving to a kindergarten class.

In these, and other situational pictures, the child identifies himself in relation to others. The learner becomes involved when real emotions and responses are portrayed.

Newspaper pictures capture the immediacy of an event, and are often useful in pointing up a discussion. Picture magazines have similar pictures and these are on slick paper, which makes them clearer. A useful resource file can be made by a teacher (or a church school committee) willing to take the time to look through selected magazines with an eye to pictures which deal with areas to be found in the curriculum. Pictures of family life are relevant, as are pictures of the natural world, whether of spring beauty or the violence of storms, and pictures of children in school or on the streets.

However, the stereotyped posed pictures which make up the bulk of the glamorous multicolor advertising pictures have nothing to offer. They are artificial and therefore they say nothing honest. The children are too beautiful, the mother is too undisturbed, the house is too perfect. It would be cruel to use such pictures at all in some situations. They are irrelevant in most situations, and therefore are not even useful as decoration.

*Cartoons.* Cartoons are a valuable teaching aid, for they are commentaries on life. In addition to those in the newspapers, the cartoons which enliven the women's magazines and which, in a sophisticated form, are the staple of *The New Yorker,* may be helpful resources. The cartoon takes life seriously, but sees the humor in a situation. The people in the cartoon are very much involved in life situations, but the caption views the situation with a certain warm detachment. For this reason the cartoon is less threatening than some pictures would be. While not telling how a problem should be handled, cartoons suggest that there are possibilities for solution short of an explosive climax in the lives of families and friends.

The discovery of the value of the cartoon in teaching has been a recent one and you will notice both the individual picture and the cartoon strip being used from time to time. Let it suggest that you keep your eyes open as you read the magazines which come to your home. If you are a library reader and something catches your eye, you will find a newsstand copy an inexpensive investment toward the enrichment of teaching.

## Other Forms of Art

*Stained-Glass.* There are forms of art in each church building, and in other areas of the community. Sometimes teachers overlook this fact. Have you stained-glass windows in your church? Some of the work put into American churches in the late nineteenth century are basically glass and lead imitations of paintings, but in recent years there has been a return to the type of glass used in the European cathedrals. The deep reds and blues form a stylized picture which cannot be clearly delineated at a glance, but must be looked at thoughtfully until the scene it represents grows clear and the viewer begins to reflect on the meaning. Contemporary churches have increased the range of colors used, adding deep violets and glowing yellows. Abstract art has been introduced so that each person who looks at the window may interpret the meaning of event or symbol as he sees it.

*Decorative Arts.* Some churches are planned in Byzantine style and have mosaics. These are stylized pictures of biblical events made in small pieces of tile. They originated in the Eastern churches in the fifth to the twelfth centuries. Lovely reproductions of some of the original mosaics may be found in art picture books.

The stylized artistry of the ikon, or holy pictures, is found in the churches of Eastern Christendom. These also have been reproduced in color pictures. Some churches contain frescos—molded plaster figures which are raised slightly from the wall on which they are placed. These are three-dimensional. Wood carving, especially around a pulpit or in an altar reredos, is similar in nature.

Sculpture has been minimized in the church since the Reformation, for it has often seemed to suggest a "graven image." Plaster and even marble statuary, whether of American or Mediterranean origin, has often been sweetly sentimental, hardly suggesting the rugged character of biblical figures. Contemporary sculpture, preferring rough forms and varied materials, has often been a more satisfactory vehicle for expressing the meaning of the Christian faith. Visitors to the new cathedral at Coventry, England, have been impressed by the various forms which the contemporary expression of the Christian faith can take. Tapestry, bronze, wood, silver, each in its own way and at the hands of an artist, express both austerity and richness, strength and beauty. Many American communities today have at least one church in which these new forms of expression may be found, and often one may be found in your area. Museums are a source for studying Christian art. A field trip would give pupils and teacher alike some helpful insights in this area.

*Liturgical Art.* A distinction must be made between religious art and liturgical art. The artist who paints a religious picture expects it to be bought and hung in a home or
a museum, or in some room of a church. But liturgical art is
made for the express purpose of enriching the celebration of
the liturgy. Stained-glass windows have told the biblical
story of salvation. The carvings have been appropriate to
the particular part of the church in which they were used,
whether altar, baptismal font, pulpit or lectern. Thus the
objects in the church become an important form of visual
teaching for children by helping them to understand the
worship of the church. You will want them to notice where
the baptismal font is placed, its size, and how it is used. The
placing of the organ and choir should show the place of
music in the service. Look at the altar appointments. How
many candles are used, and why? What does the cross sig-
nify? Older children, during Lent, might study reproductions of crucifixes from various periods in the church's life
to see how different aspects of the Passion of our Lord are
emphasized. What is the difference between the use of a
cross or of a crucifix? What other objects are used in the
chancel? Boys and girls should have a conducted tour of the
sacristy. They can learn something of the background of the
Holy Communion vessels used today. They can be told
about the vestments in their present form, and learn about
the significance of colors and symbols used on them. The
worship of the church takes on meaning for even the younger children because it is always expressed in color, objects,
music and action as well as in words. Tours of the church
or neighboring churches should be made only when they fit
into curriculum plans or on extra-curricular time.

*Other Forms and Uses.* Study of the child's own church

can be enlarged by pictures of churches found in magazines. Picture magazines have had beautiful reproduction of historic churches of the Byzantine and Gothic periods as well as of some of the fine examples of contemporary church architecture.

These are ways of teaching through three-dimensional objects (or, where necessary, pictures of them). Other kinds of objects are useful for some units of study. Study about the church around the world will be made more vivid when the children see and touch some of the ordinary implements of everyday living in other lands. Young children are interested by clothing, shoes, and toys. Older children also like to see books. A group of younger children were fascinated when a man who had been stationed in Korea brought some souvenirs to class, and talked about some Korean children whom he had become fond of during his Army days in that country.

A vacation church school unit on the subject of "exploring God's world" indicates the kind of collection which could come from an outdoor exploration, and suggests field trips in order to appreciate those things which ought to be admired but not collected.

Archaeological treasures can help the child to see that biblical people really lived. Sometimes art collectors have ancient coins and objects that the class may see. A trip to a museum will orient a class toward ancient Egypt or Rome, according to whether one is studying the Old Testament or the New Testament. One theological seminary has a traveling collection of artifacts from ancient Israel which can bring to the children who handle the items like coins and oil lamps a sense of immediacy that no picture could ever give.

*Symbols.* Symbols are word-pictures. They are signs of

the Christian faith which will interest even the younger children. They have always seen the cross on the altar. Year by year the understanding of its meaning can be deepened. Look for symbols used on lectern bookmarks, on vestments, in windows. A course concerning Christians at worship will afford ample opportunity to explore symbols, but there are other points at which they become part of the enrichment of teaching. The Christian understanding of God as Trinity can never be understood in words, but the symbols for the Trinity—the fleur de lis, the intercircling rings, the triangle—help toward comprehending the relationships indicated in the word. Use an appropriate symbol in your room for each season of the church year, or one indicative of the current unit of study. Symbols are a part of the language of the church.

## Using Pictures

No teaching method is easier to use than pictures. A good print can be framed and placed in the room for the continual enjoyment of the class. If a group has only a corner of a room, an inexpensive print, available for purchase from many museums, can be a focal point on the screen dividing one class from another. Appreciations grow this way.

Often a teacher will want to call attention to a picture. He might place it on the bulletin board with an arrow pointing to it and a message to the children asking a question about one salient feature. The group might gather around a picture at some point in the session. Or the teacher might hold it for the class to see and ask for comments. Sometimes he might ask a specific question, "What does this picture say to you?"

A picture, especially a photograph or a cartoon, can be a discussion-starter. "What do you think happened next?" the teacher might say. Or it might be used midway in a discussion to suggest a different focus.

After discussing the possibilities in a cartoon, a class could act out what they thought happened next. They might incorporate the key idea into a role-play situation revolving around what went before as well as what might happen.

When used to illustrate a story, a picture should be shown at a point appropriate to the scene it depicts. Often teachers have held up a teaching picture which told the end of the story and then proceeded to start at the beginning! They had thereby brought the children to the ending before giving a chance to experience the whole episode.

Pictures may also be a springboard for writing. A picture, particularly a realistic photograph, can suggest a story to a child. The first-graders like to tell their story to a teacher who prints it on a large sheet of paper for all to see. Older boys and girls are capable of composing on paper by themselves. Small reproductions of paintings might give each person a chance to make up his own story about a particular picture. Other pictures suggest the writing of poetry. Still others could inspire a meditation.

### Projected Visual Resources

Projected visual materials are widely used in church school teaching. Motion pictures, filmstrips (with and without recordings), film clips, and view-master reels are all being used. The advancing technology of both film and projection-equipment manufacturers holds out the promise of still other types of projected audio-visuals in the near future.

One such development is a four-minute, 8 mm, motion picture clip, pre-loaded in a cartridge for convenient use with newly devised, inexpensive projectors.

The use of projected audio-visuals is a major teaching method in many church school curricula today. Especially designed and prepared audio-visual materials are a part of teaching suggestions for Sunday, weekday, and vacation church schools. These filmstrips may illumine the background of a particular biblical period such as that of the Roman Empire at the birth of Christ. They may explain the service of worship in such a way as to start the teacher and class on their own discussion of the elements in the service. They can tell the story of a life in vivid capsule form. They can illustrate the work of the church in one particular area of mission. These filmstrips correlate with story and discussion materials provided in a unit of study. They convey to children (and adults) situations which could never be conveyed by word alone.

Filmstrips to be used in curriculum are both "sound" and "silent." Sometimes, as you will note in use, background sound effects and music add much to the drama of the story being told. At other times, a filmstrip can be a more useful teaching-learning tool if the pace at which it is shown is not controlled by a recording. A study of the meaning of symbols would be this kind of a filmstrip. Symbols have a natural fascination for junior age boys and girls. Rather than a recording or reading script, such a filmstrip provides the teacher with a discusion guide. As the pictures are projected, the teacher draws responses from pupils and builds on their reactions and questions. The rate at which the pictures are projected is controlled completely by the teacher. The result is a dynamic learning experience rather than just the running through of a filmstrip. Discussion takes place as the message of the filmstrip unfolds rather than at its conclusion.

Specific directions for use of projected audio-visuals are provided in course teacher's guides and in the leader's guides accompanying each audio-visual item. Sometimes a filmstrip is used to introduce a unit of study. More often it is used at or near the end of a unit to summarize and bring together other learnings. This could happen through the use of a filmstrip on how the world began. The unit might be devoted to how we understand the work of God the Creator in relationship to what we have learned about the physical world. The filmstrip provides a sweeping overview of the long span of the world's development and conveys something of the drama and wonder of this magnificent story. Pupils have studied many facts about the world both in public and church schools. The filmstrip helps to relate these pieces of knowledge.

Filmstrips are most often used as one step in a series of learning experiences within a unit. This means that what precedes and what follows the actual projection of the filmstrip is often as important as the viewing itself. One example of a thoroughly integrated use of a filmstrip could be used in a course on the Old Testament prophets. The filmstrip is about Amos, spokesman for God. Below is an outline of the suggested use of the filmstrip in one unit on Amos.

1) Prepare pupils for use of the filmstrip. Here is one plan to follow:

   a) Write questions about Amos suggested in the course teacher's guide on the chalkboard. Add any questions pupils may raise.

b) Divide the class into research groups.

c) Assign one or more questions to each group for study.

d) Introduce the filmstrip. Explain that in it the pupils will meet a man named Amos, who was a prophet, a man who spoke for God. Explain that the filmstrip will be one resource groups may use to find answers to their assigned questions. Tell them you will show the filmstrip once all the way through. Ask them to be alert for pictures that pertain to their questions. Suggest that a group may then ask to have a frame or sequence shown again as they look for answers or share their findings with the class.

2) Show Part I (on Amos) of the filmstrip without interruption.

3) Use the filmstrip to carry out the assigned research projects. This may involve:

a) Allowing time for immediate reactions to the filmstrip and its picture of Amos and his times.

b) Reshowing any sequences pupils request to help them in their research. If your room is large and you have a table-top projector, one group at a time might use the filmstrip while other groups work with other resources, such as the Bible dictionary.

c) Providing paper or cards for note-taking. Begin the work period. Indicate other resources pupils may consult, the Reader article on Amos, passages from the Bible, a Bible dictionary. List on the chalkboard all passages that will be studied in Sessions 8 and 9 as well as Amos 8:4-6, which is used only in the filmstrip.

d) Call groups together to report on their research. Reshow any frame in the filmstrip which pupils request as an aid in discussing answers to their questions.

The way in which a filmstrip is to be used says much about the way it is to be made. While almost every filmstrip can be adapted to different uses, filmstrips, like other teaching-learning materials, are best when they are custom designed. In some of the newer curriculum materials, the place and manner of use is taken into account when each filmstrip is planned. Filmstrips, like other materials, are carefully prepared to meet certain objectives for a specific age group. Thus, projected audio-visuals take their place along with other teaching-learning tools and methods.

Projected audio-visuals for the parish education curriculum are confined chiefly to filmstrips and sound filmstrips. These have been chosen because of their proven effectiveness as teaching-learning tools, their economy to the user and their suitability for use in church school classes. Motion pictures, which can be highly effective teaching-learning tools, fail to meet the criteria of reasonable cost and suitability of use.

Most motion pictures are far too expensive to be purchased by church schools. Even on a rental basis, the typical eight- to twelve-dollar cost per showing is greater than many budgets will permit. Perhaps even more serious are the difficulties encountered in using motion pictures in the church school. Most motion pictures are at least fifteen minutes in length. Many are longer, with some even running for forty-five minutes. Rare indeed is the motion picture so valuable that it is worth half, three-quarters, or all of a session! A skilled teacher who uses a variety of teaching-learning methods will not want to limit very many sessions to this one method. There are also the added difficulties due to the fact that motion pictures require expensive projection equipment, the operation of which is not familiar to many church school teachers. A completely independent classroom which can be darkened is a must for use of motion pictures.

By contrast, filmstrips can be used in any church school situation, even in a large room where many classes meet side by side with no sight or sound barriers between them. Newly developed table-top projectors and screens are inexpensive, easily operated and highly portable. They can be used with complete satisfaction with no darkening of the class meeting area. Any teacher can use a filmstrip with table-top projection equipment with no more disturbance to neighboring classes than holding up a picture and talking about it.

*Opaque and Overhead Projectors.* Opaque and overhead projectors are two devices for projection teaching-learning materials with which church school teachers should be familiar. Both are expensive ($125 and up for overheads; from $250 for opaques). But both are highly useful and should be found among the tools available in a well equipped church school. An opaque projector will project virtually anything: a newspaper clipping, a cartoon, a picture cut from a magazine. A newspaper clipping is far too small to be read by everyone if just held up. Passing it around the class is time-consuming and results in a loss of interest on the part of pupils. But projected through an opaque projector, the same clipping can be read by everyone with the attention and interest of all being directed to the same spot.

An overhead projector makes use of specially-prepared

transparencies. Virtually anything may be drawn or copied onto a transparency. (However, the equipment needed for making transparencies is at least as expensive as the projector itself.) A teacher may write on a transparency with a grease pencil, or by using acetate overlays may appear to write on the transparency while actually preserving it for subsequent use. Transparencies may be kept, filed, and used again and again. The primary advantage of the overhead projector is that the teacher gains all the utility of a chalkboard, tackboard, and charts but never loses eye-contact with pupils. Whatever the teacher chooses to put on the overhead projector appears instantly on the wall over his head where every pupil can see it, but the teacher never has to turn away from the class to write or to point out something of interest.

## Other Visual Materials

Other kinds of visual materials are helpful in giving the boys and girls background for their study. Maps help them to visualize the size and contours of a country, the travels of biblical people, and so on. Charts put material in a compact form which they can look at long enough even to memorize. A chart with the Lord's Prayer, the Ten Commandments or the Creed help a class to memorize. Class discussion can then center in interpretation. Lists outlining the unit or summarizing a study are helpful.

Nor should one neglect the possibilities of the bulletin board. Most teachers use this for displaying the children's work. It can also be used for presenting and explaining the material in a unit. The range of useable materials is vast. There can be a three-dimensional display employing objects, wood, metal, cloth. The class—or class committees—could be responsible for displays. This is a skill which a teacher would do well to develop. The chalkboard, the flip-chart, large turn-over paper tablets set on easels, and other visual materials should not be overlooked.

Where do you find all these materials? At first, you will have to remember to look for them. Later, you will find that your first impulse in looking at a newspaper or magazine is to ask, "What can I use in my class?" You will be looking at store displays and saying, "Here is an idea I could use."

Visual materials will be used whenever a class meets. Pupils are going to be looking at something. You can help decide what they will see.

# 5. Listening to Music and Poetry

WHEN children listen in church school, they usually hear the spoken word. But the ear is attuned to varying kinds of sounds and the child needs to hear music and the rhythms of poetry as well as prose stories and explanations. Too often we think of music as useful only for relaxation (as in a singing game), as practice for worship, or in the worship service itself. By so doing, we neglect a whole area for the enrichment of teaching.

In music, the child learns through sounds which evoke

response and express feelings: joy, sadness, resolution. Music is an expression of faith in which children can share.

A children's choir participated in a production of Benjamin Britten's opera "Noe's Fludde." They were the animals, and their role was denoted by the masks they wore. Their part was simple. They entered the ark, two by two, singing "Kyrie Eleison" and they left singing "Alleluia." They sang with the whole cast and congregation the hymn which asks that Christ who calmed the sea would "hear us when we cry to thee for those in peril on the sea." By their participation in this musical event, they gained a depth of insight into the story of the Flood that few church school teachers would think to give them. They began to see that to the Christian church, the ark is a symbol of salvation, that participation in the Christian life is a going from death (Kyrie Eleison) to resurrection (Alleluia). The story of Noah's Ark is no longer a nursery tale to boys and girls who have seen it treated more profoundly. Whether the reference be back from the calming of the storm to the Flood, or forward from the Flood to the New Testament references to Jesus on the sea of Galilee, this is an enrichment of biblical study. The records are available, as is the medieval play from which the words are taken. The point of the illustration, however, is not to have teachers run out to use this piece, but rather to point out that various classical works of music are usable with children.

## Hymns in Teaching

Hymns express the faith of the church. Children are given an opportunity to participate in this faith as they learn to sing hymns.

The oldest hymns of the church are contained in the psalms. There are many opportunities for using these in teaching. The obvious time is when a particular study of the book is being made, but this does not begin to exhaust the possibilities. Many of the psalms recount the history of Israel, especially the story of the Exodus and the conquest of their Promised Land. These can be used during Old Testament study. Others, songs in praise of God's creative and providential work, will enrich the units in that area which a class is studying. Others are prayers for help, or assurances of confidence in God. These are helpful when talking about the needs of the children and their relationship to God. Other psalms are reflections of the worship of the Temple and can be used in a study of the worship of the church.

We are speaking here primarily of the singing of psalms, although a knowledge of the meaning of the words precedes singing them. Many psalms have been set to music. Also many hymns are psalm paraphrases (for a list, consult the hymnal index). Many of these, the Genevan and Scottish psalm tunes, arose out of the early Reformed Church. They are among the finest types of hymn tune because of their dignity and simple rhythm. Young children learn these with ease. You will find some of them in the various new children's hymnals being published by several denominations. We sometimes forget that the psalms were originally written to be sung, although we do not know precisely what kind of music was used to go with them. Much present practice in psalm-singing goes back to the plainsong or Gregorian chant of the Middle Ages. Sixth graders would be interested in the early and contemporary forms of the chant. Actually these are easy to learn because they follow an easily recognized pattern and are really a rhythmical "reading" of the words. One of the most familiar examples of plainsong in our hymnals is "O Come, O Come, Emmanuel."

The New Testament also contains hymns, such as Mary's song, the *Magnificat*, "My soul doth magnify the Lord" (Luke 1:46-55); Simeon's song, the *Nunc Dimittis*, "Lord, now lettest thou thy servant depart in peace" (Luke 2:29-32); and others. The early Christians sang from the Jewish Psalter, adding songs of their own for their worship. Children can pick these up in their study of New Testament materials and in seasonal emphases. Some will come up in a study of the worship of the church. These hymns, too, have been put to musical settings. Look in the author index of your hymnal and you will find some of the oldest Christian hymns in use.

Some parts of the liturgy come from the early centuries of the church. The *Te Deum*, "We praise thee, O God," is a great hymn of praise; Christians, as they sing it, know themselves to be linked with prophets, apostles, and martyrs. The hymnals contain a number of hymns written in the early centuries. (Tunes usually come from later times.) Teachers who are working with units of study in church history should be aware of this resource. Hymn verses, like other forms of poetry, reflect the thoughts and feelings of the writers. So the study of a hymn gives an insight into the historical character or time being studied. It also helps in understanding the ways in which the Christian community expressed its faith in different centuries. One can understand the Protestant Reformation better by knowing "A Mighty Fortress."

A study of hymns helps to enrich the study of the Bible

(notice the biblical references in many hymns) as well as the history, theology, and worship of the church. They help the child to express his own relationship to God. They can be used to voice his prayer in time of need, and to state his assurance of God's love. They suggest a depth to study which might otherwise be overlooked: the solemn mood of the Advent hymns, for example, or the linkage of the Passover with the Resurrection in the Easter hymns.

Sometimes you will want to use only the words of a hymn, either because the music is beyond the range of the children, or because you are in a setting where singing would be inconvenient. Studying the words is a necessary beginning to the learning of any hymn because the purpose of the music is to carry the meaning of the words. Let the boys and girls read the words silently. Ask what words are unfamiliar, and think of the meaning. Talk about what the hymn is trying to say. Listen to the music and see how it fits the words. Then begin learning to sing it. With first- and second-graders the approach will be different. You will want to read the hymns aloud, even if they are following words printed on the chalkboard, on a chart, or in a book. Pick out difficult words for them to pronounce with you and tell them the meaning. Ask them what they think the hymn is trying to say. Then let them listen to the hymn being sung and finally ask them to follow along as they begin to learn it. Soon they will be singing confidently, learning whole phrases and catching the rhythm of the lines, carried along by the participation of the whole group.

The musical accompaniment for hymns may vary widely. Almost any teacher can sing a hymn in teaching children, once it is realized that children are not critics and that a teacher can carry a tune better than most children. If a piano or organ is available in an assembly room or chapel, take the children there and have someone play the melody with one hand. Many people do not realize that in order to learn a tune clearly, children need to hear it uncluttered by accompaniment. That can be added later. Having a piano in a classroom is not necessary; in fact, it takes up room which can be better used in other ways.

Many teachers today are discovering the value of recordings as a means of worship and music instruction. Curriculum suggestions for a course will include among audio-visual resources a number of recordings at various age levels to serve as companion teaching aids and to provide enriching listening opportunities for the great heritage of Christian hymnody and church music. These will often be selections from the children's hymnal, sung by children's voices, and planned to aid the teacher in the instruction of hymn-singing. Other records may include an entire church service and be of value in helping a class see the movement of the parts of the service as well as providing the opportunity of interrupting the service at particular points in order to talk about its meaning. Such listening can also help a class of younger children develop their skills in participating in responsive readings.

## Listening to Religious Music

Hymns are not the only forms of religious music which can be used in teaching. The Christian faith has been proclaimed and the feelings of Christians about their faith have been expressed in many forms of music. Children need to hear some of these for appreciation. We should not leave to the public schools the task of preserving this heritage.

It will be lost in the wide range of music to which they wish to introduce the child.

One thinks first of the distinctively American heritage of the Southern mountain music, and even more important, the Negro spirituals. Here were a people profoundly sensitive to what the Bible was saying about slavery and freedom, man's oppression and God's grace. Boys and girls should learn these spirituals as they study the Bible, and they should also have an opportunity simply to listen to them. The recordings of Marian Anderson are suggested, or the singing of Leontyne Price, or the music of a fine Negro choir. These have much to say about the meaning of the biblical faith.

Oratorios are a combination of music and words in solos, choruses, and recitative. Many of these use religious subjects, although they were written for general public performance and not for congregational liturgical use. A class studying the Creation narratives might well listen to a recording from Haydn's oratorio, "The Creation." Selections from Handel's "Messiah" provide commentary on the Christmas or Easter season. Twentieth-century music has made some notable additions to the library of Christian music: Honegger's "King David," Britten's "St. Nicholas," Pierne's "The Children's Crusade." Teachers will be able to find records through the public library, or by inquiring among members of the parish who have collections. Use borrowed records only with first-rate needles and good equipment.

The greatest writer of church music is conceded by almost all to be Johann Sebastian Bach. His cantatas were written to be used in the service and for this reason they have a different focus than religious compositions written for the general public. They are expressions of faith by one who shares the faith. They are a witness to the Christian faith being made within the congregation of the faithful. The singer is involved in what he is saying.

Look, for example, at Cantata 140, "Sleepers, Wake, a Voice Is Calling." This is an Advent cantata, based on the Gospel parable of the wise and the foolish virgins and on the Advent hymn by Philip Nicolai, "Wake, Awake, for Night Is Flying." In a Bach cantata, the opening chorus sets the theme, but the solos or duets which follow are arias in which the person, confronted by Christ, makes his response as a cry for help and an assurance of acceptance. In this cantata, the petition comes in a duet, "Whence comest thou, my Lord? . . . I open the hall . . . come, Jesu!" And the assurance comes later, "Yes, I am thine. My love no power can sever." The final chorale is always a great psalm of praise.*

This particular cantata is analyzed only by way of illustration. You may find others more suitable to your class. Many libraries have examples of the cantatas, and music-lovers often include them in their own collections. Bach's Passion music, "The Passion according to St. Matthew" and "The Passion according to St. John" not only have arias which you would find helpful in deepening the awareness of the boys and girls in the understanding of the Crucifixion, but also chorales which give voice to the Christian's devotion to Christ, his Savior. Several of these chorales are also used in the hymnal. When you are studying the worship of the church, look at the "Mass in B Minor" to see where it can be helpful. The music of the "Credo" is itself a magnificent commentary on the creed. To hear the haunting sorrow of the "Crucifixus," followed immediately by the leap-

* Cantata 140, recorded under the auspices of the Bach Guild. Vanguard (BG-598).

ing joy of the "Resurrexit," is to grasp the totality of the redemptive event and to understand why Christians call that Friday "good."

There are many recordings of liturgy to help older boys and girls understand the worship of their own church. Well-trained choral groups such as the Shaw Chorale have recorded hymns, including special discs for Christmas and for Easter. Choose the best hymnody for children's listening. The chanting of psalms by a synagogue choir will introduce them to the Old Testament roots of the faith. Music from an Orthodox Liturgy will give them some of the worship atmosphere of the Eastern churches. Listening to parts of the Mass, using plainsong, will make them acquainted with the worship of the pre-Reformation church or the continuing Roman Catholic tradition. The Taizé brothers in France, a monastic community of the Reformed Church, has produced contemporary forms for the liturgy and recorded these.

"When are we to find time for this?" you ask. Perhaps you will not find time. Perhaps the lesson plans and learning experiences suggested in your teacher's guides will give you all the help you ever need. But a moment may arrive—some special event, some personal reason—when a different method or different resource will be most helpful. If such a moment comes, you will want to be ready to use that which is best for the occasion. The more knowledge, facility, and experience a teacher has, the better he can adapt lesson plans to fit his pupils' learning needs as well as his own teaching talents.

Often you may feel justified in using recordings in the background of your work. A record might be playing as the early-comers arrive in class. Recordings are particularly useful while a class is engaged in an activity. Children seem able to do two things at once. In fact, many people find that listening to music releases their thoughts so that they do better work with a radio or phonograph on. Do not think you are slighting the music if you do this. A recording of Easter hymns is a good background for the making of an Easter mural, and a recording of the opening chorus of the "St. Matthew Passion" could help a class writing on the significance of the entrance into Jerusalem (with reference to Advent as well as to Holy Week). If you do not have a room of your own, you will need to make special provision to meet somewhere occasionally where music can be played.

If there is some special musical event in your church you will want to suggest to the children that they attend with their families. You might even talk about it in class on the following week. Sometime you might ask the organist to play for your class, if he is free during the time that the church school meets. He might play a hymn which they have been learning, showing them the different ways in which it can be played, and sharing part of a chorale prelude based upon the hymn. He could help them to learn a new response. This gives the children an opportunity to get to know him (some may already know him from choir), makes them acquainted with the workings of the organ— that wonderful accompaniment for the worship of the church—and broadens the areas of teaching methods.

When the boys and girls attend the church service, direct them toward sympathetic listening. Talk with them about the purpose of the prelude and postlude, and the differing mood of each. Notice the points at which choral music is used, what music is used and when the congregation participates. Think about the meaning of the musical part of The Offertory.

This is part of the training for participation in the worship of the church, which is an important objective for each age group within a curriculum. The curriculum has courses and sessions which give direct opportunity for instruction in worship and music. To supplement the instruction that the classroom teacher may offer, a music adviser may offer guidance to classroom teachers to help them improve their own leadership skills in worship and music instruction. He may also work directly with groups of children by coming to their class or department for the specific purposes of teaching them hymns and other choral elements of the service.

## Listening to Poetry

Poetry, like music, can be appreciated without being completely understood. Indeed, an elaborate analysis which tries to extract the meaning from every word and phrase is deadening. Poetry has music and rhythm. It expresses emotion. It evokes moods. Poetry is not so much a description of events as a commentary on them. The poet is using sounds and images differently from the way most of us do. If we take the trouble to orient ourselves to his writing, we may have a new slant on life. Poetry can be a rich medium for the children's learning when their teacher is himself fond of poetry and finds joy in sharing this pleasure with children.

Good children's verse is one form of poetry. Written by persons sensitive to children, it expresses the longings of the child and comments on his relationship to persons and to the world. Dorothy Aldis, Elizabeth Maddox Roberts, and A. A. Milne, among others, have done this. Robert Louis Stevenson caught the moods of children in his poems. So did Christina Rossetti, writing earlier in the nineteenth century; no one more adequately than she has expressed a child's wonder at the natural world. Poets who do not write primarily for children have sometimes addressed themselves to the child's world. How does one find these poems? There are few collections of poetry with religious insights to use with children. A teacher may have to make a collection by spending a few pleasant hours in the library, especially scanning anthologies of poetry for children. Except for Christmas poetry, which deals with the event itself, most of the verse will express the feelings and responses of children to their own experiences, to the people around them, and the world.

Poetry can be used as a discussion-starter. After reading a passage, the teacher might say, "Have you ever felt this way?" or "Does this describe anything you have ever thought?" or "What do you suppose made the writer say this?" It can be used at the ending of a discussion to sum up the feeling left by the subject under consideration: "We have delved into the scientific theories about Creation and we have talked about the biblical view of Creation; here is how a poet feels about it." The teacher needs to remember that, as in other areas, not all poetry about God or man reflects Christian beliefs. Care should be taken in the selection. Care, too, should be taken in trying to pick reasonably good poetry. A lot of doggerel gets into print. As with pictures and music—and most everything else—familiarity with works generally conceded to be classic is the best way of learning how to judge the literary worth of a poem, picture, or composition.

Poetry can be used to describe a situation or to give one's reaction to a situation. It invites further comment. It can also be used for simple enjoyment. It does not have to fit into a pattern. Read a poem while the younger children are at activity work. Or, read it and let them make a picture to illustrate it. Make a booklet of poems for Christmas or a booklet of poems about the world God has made. Illustrate the books.

There is poetry in the Bible. The psalms and the early Christian hymns mentioned earlier are poems even though they may not rhyme. Some of the early traditions of the Old Testament are in verse, and are so shown in the Revised Standard Version. Older children would enjoy listening to parts of the Song of Moses (Exodus 15), or the Song of Deborah (Judges 5) or David's lament over his friend Jonathan (2 Samuel 1:17-27).

We have been talking about poetry read by the teacher, There is also a place for asking a child who enjoys poetry to read to the class. We shall not ask them to prepare poetry for a "performance." Most poetry can most effectively speak when used informally and naturally.

Some poetry can be used as a form of choral reading by the whole group. Poems which lend themselves easily to this kind of treatment have dialogue and narration. Some will have a refrain which can be taken by the whole group, while individuals or smaller groups speak the rest of a stanza. Such a carefully prepared use of poetry suggests its being presented to a wider group, a special assembly, or to visiting parents.

# 6. Studying and Thinking

THE Bible speaks of loving God "with all your mind" and in part this means that the mind of man, created by God, is to be developed in his service.

The mind is to be used to deepen the understanding of who God is and how one serves him.

Intelligence has a function in religious learning. The early Christians were admonished to be able "to give a reason for the faith that is in you." The use of reason as a

God-given faculty has always been encouraged in the mainstream of the life of the church. A simple faith does not mean an ignorant faith or one that represses intellectual curiosity. The Bible contains many manuscripts, all of which were carefully written and compiled. The writers were intelligent as well as religious, careful in learned skills as well as spiritually perceptive.

Religious faith has always attracted scholars, who have spent lifetimes pondering the deeper meanings of the biblical insights. The commentaries on the Law, written by Jewish scholars before the time of Christ, covered many volumes. The first biblical scholar in the Christian tradition was Origen, who lived and wrote in the middle of the second century. Two hundred and fifty years later, another scholar, Jerome, translated the Bible from the original languages into Latin, the language spoken in his day. Through the centuries the list has grown.

It is as true for teachers and pupils today as it has ever been in the past, that research can stimulate thought. Learning is not an easy process, even for those who enjoy studying, yet learning breeds learning. Research is a process which we have seldom taken seriously in the church school. Intensive study should be part of all kinds of education, both religious and secular. Boys and girls are used to it at an early age in their public school experience, but several factors have been combined to make it a neglected area of religious education. Perhaps the teacher has never done this kind of digging into the meaning of the biblical faith and Christian life, and hesitates to let the class begin lest questions arise which he might find difficult to answer. Such a teacher should remember that Christian learning is a joint enterprise between pupils and teacher and that the teacher is not to act as an infallible authority, but as a Christian growing in grace and in understanding. Another point of hesitation lies in the brief period so often available for church school. In this case, the practical solution might lie in narrowing the area of research and distributing sections to different pupils.

Problem-solving is superficial if it is based only on a sharing of present experiences by immediate contemporaries. It reaches deeper levels only when the experience of many others from distant past and near past are used to shed light on the possibilities. To be sure, each person is unique, yet each shares certain elements of experience in common with others. New insights come when a person, looking at the possibilities for solutions within the lives of others, transmutes their experience into his own life's situations. This kind of problem-solving can be done through thoughtful research, study, and thinking.

## Methods Used in Research: Tools of Learning

The most obvious research tool is the pupil's reading book, where there is one. Most often the reader will supply narrative material or open-ended stories that are to be used during a session's study. The material should usually be used as suggested. But when there is special time or interest, such material may also be used for research. Then there will be a change in the way you use it. You will ask the class to read a story, or a section, keeping certain points in mind, or looking for the answer to one or more questions which you will expect to discuss after all have finished the reading.

For example, when a class is reading about the prophet

Amos, you might say, "As you reread the story of Amos, be ready to reconstruct for us a picture of religious conditions in his time in Israel." This helps the boys and girls to concentrate on getting a vivid picture of the situation which Amos spoke about. You could continue by asking if they have observed (from newspapers, adult conversations, their own experience) any similar conditions in the religious situation of our own day. The class is now ready to dig into the message which the prophet Amos addressed to his people. A story for younger children might be used as the basis for study about the way other people live. Even second-graders could do some thinking about why a migrant people became uprooted, or what Johnny and Sally found life in the big city to be like.

The second research tool ready at hand may be the pupil's workbook or activity sheets integrated with the units of study. It asks the pupil to think about and write responses to the material. It gives questions to answer, statements to reflect upon, sentences to complete. The child is thus given a specific way of clarifying his learning. Your teacher's guide will suggest points in the session plan at which to use the material, but you will sometimes find it better to place it elsewhere. If you are crowded for time one day, carry over this kind of activity to the beginning of the following session as review. Do not feel bound by a necessity to finish the material at each session; let each child move at his own rate. The suggestions in the teacher's guide are best for most classes, but there will be times, occasionally, when your class is not typical.

Although all essential materials are built into the curriculum, enrichment materials are often available. Boys and girls are accustomed to using resource books in school.

An authoritative study on the pre-adolescent says of boys and girls in the ages from nine to twelve: "These children learn with little difficulty to use source materials—dictionaries, encyclopaedias, maps, indices, etc."[*]

Keep on hand picture articles from magazines such as the *National Geographic* which can provide background information on whatever pupils are studying. The church library probably has one or more picture books on the Holy Land. Keep available an inexpensive picture-atlas, of which several, both in hard covers and paperbacks, are now available. Some boys and girls, even without a suggestion from the teacher, may get up and consult the atlas in response to an inquiry about the land of Israel and its people. The several picture dictionaries available are most suitable for Grades 3 and 4, but can still be helpful with older boys and girls. Word books help them to probe theological meanings of words. Where you have fifth- and sixth-graders from an intellectually privileged background, you can begin to introduce them to adult Bible dictionaries and word books, for they will like to see the wealth of learning available as a promise of what they can later study, even if much of it is beyond their immediate comprehension. Children like to have their minds stretched but do not want to have the process insisted upon to the point of boredom. On the other hand, if they are not asked to probe with some depth and accuracy, they conclude that, in contrast with the work in public school, the content of the Christian faith does not encourage thought and discovery.

An adequate set of large, clearly-marked maps is a help

[*] Arthur Witt Blair and Willam H. Burton, *Growth and Development of the Preadolescent*. (New York: Appleton-Century-Crofts, 1951).

for any church school class. However, materials that are needed are usually supplied with the course material. Pupil's readers and workbooks usually include helpful maps and charts. The story the Bible tells does not concern an imaginary land, but one with firm geographical foundations. The places may have different names today, and the glory of ancient empires has departed, but they are still visible on the maps. Maps help boys and girls to locate cities, to trace journeys and distance, and to see the contour of the land in such a way as to help an understanding of climate, living conditions, and the occupations of the people.

Charts are a mainstay of the public school teacher, and the church school teacher will find them equally helpful. A chart gives pertinent events at a glance. It serves as a quick point of review, and its constant visible presence on a wall is an aid to learning. Almost without realizing it, the children see the words and absorb the contents. In this way, many have learned a psalm, or a biblical passage (such as the Beatitudes or the Ten Commandments), or a prayer. The visitor to a church school room should be able to tell at a glance what has been happening by the material in capsule form which the charts convey. Not all charts have to be in writing. Graphs are enjoyed by children. Posters point up key ideas. The possibilities within this type of visual resource material are almost unlimited. The boys and girls (at least of upper grades) can personally make most of this material. Thus learning takes place at two points, as an expression of research, and as a reminder for recall.

Some kinds of filmstrips and slides come properly under the heading of research tools. There are several excellent sets of filmstrips on the geography of the Holy Land and on the life and customs of Bible times. The size of the projected picture makes it easily useable with a whole class if a separate room which can be darkened is available.

Such a filmstrip should not be run through hastily, as one would a story strip, but is rather to be lingered over, pausing to look at details where the children wish, or skipping over pictures that have no particular value to any present study. Although such material is usually shown to fourth graders and older, a teacher showed a color strip on the Holy Land to a second grade class and they were fascinated. It was a vivid opening for a unit of stories from the life of Jesus. Similarly, a filmstrip or a brief movie on the subject of soil erosion might illuminate a discussion of man's stewardship of land.

There are a number of excellent picture books which can be used in a similar way. Although expensive, they are useful in ways where the projected picture has limitations. A book may be consulted casually, at any time; it may be used in the light; is available to one child while the rest may do something else; it can be used for pre-session or post-session continued research, and can be suggestive for written or graphic work by the pupil.

## "Live" Methods of Research

People can be drawn upon as resources, too, and we often neglect the possibilities of face-to-face learning. The teacher is the primary resource, but he usually finds himself the guide who plans the work and stands by for moment-to-moment guidance. At a particular point he might say, "I guess we need to look that up somewhere. I have a book at home which will help. I'll see what I can find out by our next class." At the next session he would give a brief presentation that invites further inquiry from the class. Or he might say, "You want to know more about how our church works. Why don't we have a question-and-answer period? I will share with you what I know." Again he becomes the center of the discussion in a pointed way and for a limited time. This is quite different from the kind of procedure in which the teacher does most of the talking in a class period without even being conscious of the fact. It serves to safeguard the class from the role of passive listening, because they are taking the initiative in asking for specific information.

At other times, however, it is helpful to have an outside person, another voice, act as resource. The minister comes to tell about his work; another church member describes how the parish reaches out into the community; someone who has lived abroad tells about the church in that country; a parent presents his side of "getting along with our family." The resource person should not be invited until the subject has been opened and some preparatory study has been made. Then the class will have background and will have formed some questions to be asked. Sometimes it is helpful to prepare in advance the questions which the class wishes to address to the resource person and to put these questions into the written invitation. The outside speaker brings a fresh approach and point of view.

First-grade children are not too young to enjoy the presence of an outside speaker. Someone must be chosen who understands children and can see events as they do. It is usually helpful if, instead of a presentation, there is a dialogue between the teacher and the visitor during which the former asks questions (if possible, questions which the children have already raised) and the visitor answers. The teacher can draw the children into the questioning and soon an informal learning situation develops in which the visitor feels at home and the children feel that they are learning something new and important.

Another "live" method of research is the field trip through which the pupils can see for themselves the subjects which they are studying. The first and second grades in one church school have established the custom of going to see the spring flower show once a year in the conservatory of a nearby park. They spend a few minutes at the zoo next door before leaving. One mother, who had thought that this would be just the sort of thing the children get in public school, reported with amazement that for her child this had been a real religious learning experience. She said, "He came home and told me how God had planned that each animal should be able to live. The giraffe has a long neck to get food from the trees; the zebra has stripes so that he can hide in the forest." Let it be added that the reason this was not just a pleasant outing was that the class had a teacher with not only religious perception, but with knowledge of how to prepare his class for learning before the event and how to follow up the experience wisely.

Ten-year-olds are ready for other types of field trips. Those who live near metropolitan centers can take advantage of museums and other cultural centers. An art museum will have a number of examples of religious art in the collection, and will usually arrange for a guided tour to just the points of interest needed by the group. Or an hour might be spent in the antiquities section of a museum illuminating the background of the Bible in Egypt, the Assyrian-Babylonian-Persian culture, ancient Greece or Rome. Some museums have good collections of early Christian art, and most have many examples of medieval and Renaissance ecclesiastical art. A library might be willing to show its collection of old manuscripts to help a class visualize the difficulty with which the Bible was transcribed and disseminated among the people. Often a library has examples of biblical or other religious manuscripts in various translations and languages.

If a group cannot visit an exhibit, sometimes the exhibit can come to visit them. A nearby museum might have a loan exhibit, or sometimes a theological seminary will lend coins, books, or manuscripts from its collections. It is a valuable experience for a class to take the responsibility of unpacking and setting up such an exhibit, learning about the contents and explaining these to others, and then repacking the material for the return trip. The American Bible Society has a traveling exhibit of Bibles in many languages and another exhibit of posters and pictures to illuminate the translations of the Bible. As a matter of fact, an inquiry in the congregation will almost always produce a number of Bibles in various languages, translations, and sizes which can be made into an exhibit to be shared with everyone.

A group studying about the church and its worship will want to examine their own church carefully. They may profit from visits to neighboring churches, for sometimes an understanding of one's own tradition comes by seeing it in relation to other traditions. A visit to a synagogue will bring to mind a realization of the background of our worship, for Jesus and the Twelve knew only the synagogue worship. A visit to an Orthodox church will illuminate the worship of the third and later centuries in the Eastern part of the ancient Christian world. A visit to a Roman Catholic church will show the tradition from which our church springs. It is usually helpful to ask a clergyman to explain something about his church to the children. Their own teacher has the responsibility of helping to guide the questions.

The class may be interested in getting acquainted with some of the work of outreach of their church. Those who live near certain institutions can plan a Saturday morning trip to a school, a nursery school, a center for older people, and a settlement house with its many activities. The place to be visited must be chosen carefully, keeping in mind the ability of the boys and girls to comprehend. The stress is on the way in which the agency is bringing the good news of God's love in terms of meeting the practical needs of people. The visiting boys and girls are guests, who may be simply onlookers. They will feel even more relaxed if it can be arranged for them to be participants, even if only for a few minutes, in the activities going on. For city children, a visit to a farm may be a fine way to broaden their understanding of the stewardship of God's gifts.

In a limited way, some of the methods of group presentation used with young people and adults may be introduced with fifth- and sixth-graders. Ask three of the boys and girls who have inquiring minds and are talkative to do a little preparatory reading and thinking and then discuss what they have read. They do this before the entire class, who do not at first join the discussion. The subject could be the interpretation of a biblical story, a question of Christian living, or the possible endings to an open-ended story. (This is technically called a symposium.) After the three have had an initial time (perhaps five minutes) in which to explore the question among themselves, the discussion is opened up to the questions and comments of the whole group. This technique has the value of giving the voluble ones a legitimate exercise of their talents for talking, and encourages the others to become involved after a while.

A variant is the panel, in which a few pupils who are willing to do a little work prepare themselves on several aspects of a study. Each in turn makes a brief presentation; they ask each other questions, and then the whole group is invited to participate. The difference between a panel and a symposium is that panel members each represent a distinct point of view or an area of research, whereas in a symposium there can be overlapping of interests. Also, a panel is slightly more formal. When studying the call of the Twelve, panel members might give brief portraits of several of the disciples, then discuss how these men differed in abilities to present the teachings of Jesus. Or the study of the prophets might include brief presentations of some of the prophets not taken up in the pupil's book. This kind of report enriches the learning of the whole class through the research of a few who are able to do the work. Panels could also speak on topics like "How we prepare for Christmas," or "Difficulties in being Christian at school."

These methods cannot be used often, but if used selectively to encourage and stimulate study discussion for the rest of the class, they have a value. Boys and girls are accustomed to being given intellectual goals in public school and will respect the need for using their minds to comprehend the interests of church and faith.

## Memorizing as a Base for Study

Memorizing is not in fashion today. Children do not learn "golden texts" nor recite passages of Scripture in exchange for cards to be exchanged later for Bibles after the manner of the trading stamps which their mothers gather. They do not often memorize poetry in school or learn a part for a school play. The time spent in memorizing is deemed better spent improvising with creative dramatics, trying to gain deeper insight into characters. They do not memorize factual material which will be readily available to them in dictionaries or other commonly used resource books. What they do memorize are the tools which they will use every day: the arithmetic tables without which they will never be able to balance the checkbook; the spelling words without which they will never be able to write a self-respecting letter. Yet many of them, even with average or above-average intelligence, fail at the little memorization that is required. With this background in mind we must inquire realistically into the place of memorization in the church school.

To begin with, some memorization should take place automatically, simply through the child's participation in the church and church school. In this manner he should learn the Lord's Prayer, the Ten Commandments, the Apostles' Creed, and probably some hymns, as well as commonly sung parts of the service (*The Gloria Patri* and *The Doxology*, for example). We must remind ourselves, however, that such memorization assures only a knowledge of the words and not of their meaning. The teacher will need to approach meanings through other methods of learning. There is a legitimate use of rote memorization when it happens in a meaningful context. But to seat a class and suggest that pupils memorize a particular passage silently, and with no particular purpose in mind, is to take all the life and meaning out of significant material and replace the learning process with boredom.

Memorization can be helpful when the material to be learned grows out of a unit of study and serves to make the whole unit more meaningful to the pupils. For example, a class studying the prophets might choose a significant verse or passage from each prophet and memorize these as a clue to understanding their messages. The history of Israel might be summed up by learning part of Psalm 136. The children might decide that it would help them in time of temptation if they could remember part of Psalm 46. One teacher has said that it helps a class to take home a typed copy of a passage to be learned, with the suggestion that it be tucked into the edge of the desk blotter or the mirror over the dresser. A few thoughtful minutes a day centered on the written material will fix it in mind by the next Sunday. The learning of catechetical material can be made easy across the weeks by a method like this. Children enjoy using little cards with material to be learned typed on them. These are carried in the pocket and looked at from time to time.

Memorization must always be seen in relation to the amount of time available for learning. Is this the best way to use the time? Sometimes it is. Some memorized material is a useful tool on which to build more thoughtful intellectual learning. Too much memorization is simply an easy way to keep a class occupied for a while, or a method of impressing parents who still nostalgically remember their own childhood, or an arbitrary way through which the facile learner may win approval. Remember that some of the most perceptive pupils find memorizing either a chore or a bore. They can think deeply and intricately, but they are understandably impatient at the time it takes to learn something someone else has said, especially if they are expected to retain such material for any length of time. Memorized material should be constantly used in order to be remembered! To learn something once and tuck it away for much later use requires a great deal of over-learning—repetition far beyond simple memorization.

## Conversation and Discussion: Exploring the "Why"

Skill in asking questions is one of the most valuable assets a teacher can develop. Sometimes he will want to ask "what, where, and when" questions to be sure that the class has some facts straight and to know that there are sound structural foundations from which to explore the "why." Most of his questions, however, will deal with this more probing area of "why." Nor dare he stop with an obvious answer. His aim should be to help boys and girls to get to the root of religious questions, whether these come from the Bible or from daily life. This means, of course, that the teacher will have at least begun to explore the roots himself. The teacher with only a superficial understanding of a subject may feel embarrassed by probing questions, whether he asks them or the children do. But the teacher should remember that learning together is not only good educational procedure but also the inevitable situation of all God's children.

The question may be "Why did Elijah oppose the priests of Baal?" It would not be enough to accept only the answer "Because they worshiped a false god." Other answers would include the fact that they were causing God's people to fall into idolatry, or more pertinently, because God's people were faithless, because they had forgotten the Covenant, because they had sinned and put themselves under the judgment of God. Going beyond that immediate event, why were they so easily led away? Was Elijah a manifestation of the mercy or the wrath of God? Are there parallel forms of idolatry which the people of God face today? Even if such questions are too advanced for young children, the teacher should think them through and, using their language, help the children see the Bible story as part of something bigger, as part of their own life.

Then there are the theological questions, which the boys and girls will raise even if the teacher doesn't. What is the meaning of Easter for us? What do we mean by eternal life? Even young children think and worry about death. They need the assurance which the Christian teacher can bring, but first they need to explore the area of their fears and concerns and to understand the questions they are really asking. A group of parents were asking how they could deal with their children's questions about life and death. It soon became apparent that the ones with religious questions were the parents themselves. They had a tendency to answer almost any question a child might ask about death in terms of "heaven." They would say "God is in heaven"; "people who die are in heaven"; "people who are good go to heaven." What "heaven" meant to the child they never questioned. It probably meant very little. The theological questions of children should not be silenced with pat answers or standard terms. When you, as a teacher, get desperate for better answers, the pastor has theological training as well as devotional insight and surely can be of help. Don't be ashamed to ask him. He knows how very little we all understand and how inexperienced we are at communicating what we know.

Sometimes you will find yourself facing questions to which the Christian witness does not always give clear answers. Boys and girls look at picture magazines, watch television, and listen to adult conversations. They want to know why God permits families to be lost in a flood, children to be burned in a tenement fire, countries to be destroyed by war. They ask why they are punished for something they did not do; why mother takes her anger out on them; why some children cheat with impunity while others are caught. The wise teacher does not have final answers. He explores these questions with the children in the light of their shared knowledge of Jesus, the biblical witness, the witness of the church.

Insight comes from the spirit and is difficult to evaluate. We do not always know the point at which an answer is sparked and a change comes about. A face brightens and someone says, "Oh, now I understand." Or a hand shoots up while an eager child yearns to share a suddenly-new answer. Real change is often imperceptible. It is only when you hear the words of a child in April and suddenly realize, startled, how different this is from what he was saying last September, that you know some change has taken place. Change, after all, is the aim of real discussion. If it stays on an intellectual level, it may be only a matching of wits or a mutual sharing of opinions. But it is possible, through rational processes, to begin a reorientation which will lead to openness to new ideas and procedures, which will be the start of new appreciations, and which may even begin a change in attitudes. Changed attitudes can lead to new ways of acting. In the final analysis, this is the work of the Holy Spirit. The teacher, to the best of his ability, has prepared the child, but God is the true teacher who sustains the child through his development and empowers him to new ways of feeling and acting.

It is important that the teacher be willing to accept as

noteworthy any sincere answer a child gives to a question, and whatever comment he makes in a discussion. This is the only way the child can freely test his thoughts and words. There is great danger in cutting a child off with sarcasm, amusement, negation, or superiority. His thoughts are important to him. Sometimes he says what he thinks in order to relieve his own feelings. Sometimes he wants to shock the teacher, or to find out what the adult reaction is to his expression of thought. There is no need always to answer. A look which accepts him is enough. (Sometimes a child doesn't really agree with his own words.) Perhaps all that is needed is a brief comment, "Tom has told us his idea on this. What would someone else like to add?" A teacher can feel that a discussion is really on its way when he becomes simply a moderator while the discussion swirls around him. Now he begins to see into the minds of his pupils. He sees through the words to the attitudes. He senses the doubts and questions. He begins to realize that pure or abstract ideas are almost nonexistent. Children philosophize in a very concrete way.

As the group discusses, the teacher begins to see the dynamic at work there. One person tends to dominate, quite without thinking; another always makes a negative comment; someone never speaks at all, but his face shows every reaction; someone else always refers his comments to the teacher. Can one work within these disparate reactions toward a common goal? It is a rewarding experience to try. It helps if an associate or team teacher can sometimes take notes on a discussion, or if very occasionally you can tape-record a class conversation. It gives you clues as to how to work through the insights of particular persons to enlarge the learning of all.

In this connection, there should be some reference to a popular method of Bible study which can be used in simple form with older grades. One takes a brief passage, incident, or story and reads it aloud while the group follows with their Bibles. Then they are given several minutes to reread it silently and to ask themselves individually, "'What is this passage saying? What is it saying to me?" Finally, the class divides into small groups (a small class stays together) while these questions are freely explored. There is no pressure on anyone to speak and no necessary follow-up on one comment by another. The aim is not to build understanding by adding the comments together; it is to gain insight by coming to an awareness of the biblical message from as many angles as there are persons participating. It can be a meaningful experience which, at the same time, is intellectual and devotional.

In a simpler way, all these techniques can be used in informal conversation with children of the first few grades. Their attention span is shorter. They want to explore the "why," but after five minutes someone will make a silly remark, and you will know that you have gone far enough for today. They will hesitate to test you with some of their ideas, and they need your encouragement in order to proceed. They will sometimes get so wrapped up in an explanation that you will have to use tactful means of eluding the details so that the main point comes through. But they are serious, these children. They have questions, and even worries, which the teacher who sees them only once a week may not note at once. Childhood is not all sunshine and light. Learning to read can be difficult; getting acquainted in a new school can be painful; having to speak before a class can be an ordeal. The freedom to share in a church school class with an understanding teacher and loving friends can give the child evidence of assurance that God, too, understands and loves.

# 7. Activity Work

THE teacher of children usually assumes that a class session is not complete without some "activity" work. In past years, this was used almost entirely at the end of class sessions and provided pupils with a way of expressing what they had learned earlier in the session. Such use of activities is indeed a valuable way to help the pupils express new understandings and new attitudes. They go from thinking to doing. Much of this chapter deals with this use of activities for it is still the chief way such projects are employed.

But it is important for the teacher to note that in recent years, and especially in new curricula being developed for church school use among most denominations, creative and constructive art or drama, music or writing, and other activities are used throughout the sessions. Sometimes they are used at the beginning of a course, to help the teacher find out how a pupil feels or thinks about something which will be discussed later. For example, first-graders in the Sunday church school start their first session by drawing something they like to do and then telling the rest of the class about it.

As for when an activity can best be used, much depends on the use to which it is to be put and the person who is going to use it. Some children get excited once they begin to use arms and legs and a measure of freedom to be creative. If they cannot quiet down easily afterwards, their teacher will want to put such activities at the end of the session, so they can work off their excitement after class. Your course teacher's guide will help you choose and schedule creative and constructive activities.

Teachers should stop to ask themselves, "Why do we do this?" Is it because the teacher's guide directs that one do so? Is it because children can sit still only for so long and need to be active? Both reasons are probably involved, but neither one explains why the time is spent on this kind of activity.

For the most part, activities come naturally after a certain point has been reached in the learning process, as attempts by the pupil to demonstrate what he has learned. In this case, they are a closing step in the learning procedure. The child begins a session by becoming involved in what is to be learned through story, visual aids, and so on. He comes to see that certain questions and information lead to decisions and commitments; he arrives at insights which come to him through study, discussion, and relationships among people. Insight brings new learning, appreciations, changed attitudes, and deepened awareness. Now the learner becomes eager to communicate to others what he has learned. He may spontaneously give his new insights expression in talking and doing, or may be guided by the teacher to choose an effective method of translating new knowledge and feeling into creative and constructive activity.

If a child is not given the opportunity to do something useful with his new insights, he will feel frustrated, and valuable learning may be dissolved or forgotten. This is why activities so often follow other methods, not necessarily at the end of a session or unit, but after new information has been gathered and new feelings engendered.

Sometimes, under the pressure of time, the teacher shortcuts the procedure. A story may not be told vividly enough to engage the child's involvment, and when a few questions are asked about it, they do not lead to any new insights. Then someone says, "Now let's draw pictures of the story." One child says, "I can't draw." Another inquires, "What shall I draw?" Someone else says, "Show me a picture." (He wants to copy it.) Two children are already at work. One is copying this neighbor's idea. Another is drawing a spaceship. What has happened? The answer is simply that the children have nothing to communicate, and they are looking for a way out of their dilemma without disappointing their teacher.

The methods which have been discussed in earlier chapters usually precede this kind of activity work. They provide factual background, intellectual content, application, and enrichment which can be drawn upon by the learner as he attempts to tell others in some way what is new to him.

The Christian must be able to explain his faith to others. He must be a witness. Sometimes a friend who is of another faith will tell of his beliefs or describe the way in which he keeps a holiday. The church school child should be able to reciprocate by explaining his beliefs and the celebrations of his church. Sometimes he will meet a child with no religious background, whose parents have neglected, avoided, or dispensed with this area of child development. How shall the believing child explain his faith in Jesus Christ and his love of God unless he has been given opportunity to put ideas into communicable form?

Then there are children who are brought up on different ethical standards. "If she hits you, you just give it back to her double," advises Mother. Or a child at school says, "My father doesn't care how I get top grades—just so that I bring home a good report." Can our children explain why they try more peaceful means of settling quarrels, or affirm,, without vaunting superiority, that their parents love them in spite of as well as because of their achievements in school? Can they explain their ethics in religious as well as in secular terms? Suppose a religious statement, made in a matter-of-fact way, meets with ridicule: "I don't believe that kind of stuff!" Will the Christian child be hurt, bewildered, angered? How can he be helped to understand such different attitudes without yielding to them? Is the brightest child in the class always correct? Is the most popular one always right?

These are the areas in everyday life for which the methods of communication try to prepare the child. Since the young child uses picture symbols more readily than words, various forms of drawing are a good beginning method.

First let us get the terms straight. When we popularly use the word "creative," we really mean "interpretative," instead. Even a great artist speaks of his "composition." Only God creates. The child takes known materials and familiar forms and by the use of insight and imagination transmutes these into different forms which express meaning for him. If they also express meaning for others, he has been able to communicate his understanding.

## The Graphic Arts

Since there are a number of forms of the graphic arts, church school teachers should not use crayons exclusively. Crayons are useful for doing large pictures, where a wide sweep of motion is indicated, a heavy outline is wanted, there are large areas to be filled in, and shading is to be suggested by light or heavy lines and filled-in areas. They are practical because they are reasonably inexpensive, always near at hand, and the children can keep clean while using them (a most important point for teachers!). Fifth-graders who are old enough not to smear powder around can do effective work with chalk. They will also like colored pencils which permit detailed work. All elementary school age children like some of the new media which keep appearing on the market. Currently there is a colored pencil which, dipped in water, acts like paint. It seems to combine the advantages of each medium. Charcoal long has been a medium of great artists. (It can get one smudged up in a hurry, though.)

Paints also can be used. A small box of water colors can be used with one or two brushes without damage to clothing. Poster paints are considered preferable by those who work in the arts with children. Poster paints do for the child what oil paints do for the adult; they give him a real feeling of freedom to express thoughts and be creative. His work will show more originality and more emotion than will the minute, careful work he does from a brush and box. When the children are provided with simple aprons and the ground rules are firmly established, the activity will result in real expressions of self. Important points to remember are that an idea of what is to be accomplished must be in mind before the first stroke is made; that each child has sufficient space in which to work comfortably; that there is adequate help at hand; and that it is understood that one brush stays in one color—no muddied paints! Obviously if your class is large and your room is crowded, you will want to use poster paints on a day when you can predict a low attendance, or at a time when you can promise that half the class will paint while the other half listens to a story (procedure to be reversed the next time). Fingerpainting, a medium requiring more imagination than skill, is more valuable for older boys and girls than has been indicated by past use. After the special paint has been applied to a glazed surface, the picture is made by using various parts of hand and finger to obtain varied results. It gives a "contemporary" feeling to painting and does not require the attention to details which so often turns the older child from paints (and crayons) with the remark, "I just can't make it look right." Younger children, too, can use it (with smocks and disposable towels).

Graphic media embrace many forms. Often teachers come to the conclusion that 9- by 12-inch paper is the best when, as a matter of fact, 12- by 18-inch paper gives more scope for development to the younger child. Posters on a background of heavy brown wrapping paper are popular, and murals—long, horizontal posters on wrapping paper or newsprint—tell a continued story.

Three-dimensional forms help to enlist the imagination of the child, who has the pleasure of choosing materials of different colors, weights, and textures for his poster. The collage can be used for retelling stories or for suggesting ideas. The collages of the artist Matisse are an example of what can be done with this medium. Figures or designs may be cut or torn from paper and mounted on another sheet to form either an appliqué or a cutout poster.

These are usually to be thought of as large-scale pieces on which several children will work at once, either with the work spread out on a long table, put on the floor, or tacked up on the wall. There is also a place for individual drawings. These may be collected in a folio, or arranged to form a book.

The important use of graphic forms lies in the ability they give the child to retell a story with interpretation, and to express feelings and situations in abstract or concrete terms. Contemporary abstract art has values for children; they will use this form if encouraged to do so. It refuses to be a camera and prefers to convey emotion, the impact of an idea on the artist. Children would gladly be released from the requirement that they be "cameras," and be told that they are free to use whatever distortion seems necessary to tell a story as they feel it. One remembers the little girl who drew Zacchaeus almost bigger than the tree in which he sat. After all, that is probably the way Zacchaeus felt at the moment Jesus spoke to him!

There are other forms of graphic method. The use of the

camera by an older child can show interpretation. Making slides can be a project engaging the skills of the older children.

Clay and plasticine are useful. Plasticine has been preferred by teachers for its "neatness" and the fact that it can be reused. Children like it for the same reasons. They have the freedom to try different forms and effects without having the material harden. Plasticine is a good medium to begin with, even if one will eventually use clay. Clay is more flexible than plasticine, but it requires the learning of a few simple skills, such as that one draws the legs and head of a figure from the body and does not attempt to attach them. (They will only fall off when the figure dries.) Working with clay has always been found to be relaxing and soothing, and seems to release the emotions and the imagination. Since form emerges from non-form, its use has always seemed closer to creativity than any other medium. One would like to see boys and girls try to convey the character of one of the disciples, or of some Old Testament figure through the form of clay. One would like to give them a word such as "atonement" or "resurrection" and see how it would be translated into this medium.

It is not necessary that the teacher be adept. Indeed, sometimes a skillful teacher will attempt to show a child how to do something and will thereby coerce the child into accepting his adult form. The teacher does need, however, to have some appreciation of the media being used so that he can encourage the child and enjoy the results of his efforts. There is no point in trying to understand all forms. One teacher might inspire excellent work in clay; another might encourage his class to reveal insights through paints.

The church school teacher will find it helpful to know

what skills are developed in the child through his public school activities. Some schools have rather elaborate facilities for crafts and have staff members who work with all children in such cases. These children will bring to church schools skills which can be tapped for the expression of Christian learning.

## Writing

The written word is another form of communication. Children begin to use this in school as early as first grade. They retell experiences to the teacher, who writes them down on chalkboard or newsprint, making the narrative from the children's contributions. For the first few school years, while the mere writing of words is a struggle, the teacher will find it better to be the children's "secretary." Obviously, the children will need to collect their thoughts before embarking on this form of activity. The experience about which they will "write" needs to be vivid.

First-graders who have been outdoors for a brief walk, or have surveyed the signs of the season from the windows of their homes have a background of experience. The next step will be a conversation through which to gather meaning from the experience. What did they see? Why do they think it happens this way? What does this show us about God? Finally the children are ready to gather their reports into written form. The theme "What we saw through the window" can be expressed in a story, a litany of thanksgiving, a letter to a friend far away. Random contributions are put into writing on the board. Then overlappings are deleted; perhaps a logical form for the composition is evolved. A final writing is made for all to see.

Not all such compositions need to be made by the group. Where there is a helping staff, stories may be gathered from individual children. Some children express themselves clearly and with originality; they want to tell about the pictures they are making. When a child has finished a drawing in some form, a teacher may ask, "Can you tell us a story about this? I will write it down for you." Then the teacher will write the child's dictated story on the back of the picture.

At what age will children be able to do creative writing themselves? You will have to watch your group and perhaps inquire of your local schools. Fourth-graders should be able to do this, but they will want to be assured that they need not be overconcerned about correct spelling. They are self-conscious about their mistakes because they know that they should be able to meet certain standards. Suggest that they write freely on the first draft, and have a dictionary handy for the final polishing.

Such writing can take many forms. From the technical standpoint, an article or essay is the simplest, for these may be written freely. "What I liked (or did not like) about the story of St. Paul"; "What the prophet Isaiah has to say to us"; "Is it hard, or easy to be a Christian at school?" A meditation is another free form of writing. The basis could be a biblical verse or passage, a collect, a special day or season in the church year.

Writing letters gives the child an opportunity to relate events in personal terms, putting himself into a situation. He can explain the worship in his church to a child in Japan or put himself in the place of a young person at some particular point in church or biblical history and write to someone else about it. Other possible letters can be from a child newly settled in the U.S.A. writing back to Germany, or from a child of the times who witnesses the actions of Jesus and tells his parents at home about it.

Stories have to follow a form and this makes them more difficult to write. If they are thought of more casually as narratives or episodes, they can be handled by boys and girls. The story tries to be an interpretation of biblical or historical events. Older boys and girls are ready to try this approach after they have read or heard imaginative stories with biblical or historical backgrounds. The intent of creative writing, however, is not merely to retell facts, but to interpret meanings. This is the point of using creative writing. The writing of a prayer can convey the significance of biblical events. Small children use the litany form easily. First establish the response: "We praise thee, O God," or "We thank thee, God, our Father," or "We pray thee, O God." Then the teacher asks the children what they wish to say. When the phrases are arranged, the pattern is established. Older boys and girls can write a litany individually. They think in personal terms, and need the opportunity to gather together and express their own thoughts and concerns.

Fourth-graders may learn the collect form of prayer. It will help them both in understanding the prayers of the church and in formulating prayer for themselves. Any unit of study on worship, the understanding of God, or biblical events will lead them into areas where they can well sum up their understandings in collect form. Although this is only one form of prayer, its orderliness helps boys and girls to focus their thoughts into meaningful phrases. They could write a prayer to be said upon entering church or one to be used at the end of the services. Each child in turn might be asked to open or close the class session with a prayer. Your teacher's guides will help you with suggestions when appropriate.

Although poetry is rarely thought of as a vehicle for children to use for the expression of religious learning, the teacher may at times encourage the class to express meanings through this form. Not all poetry needs to be rhymed, and it will be a rare child who can use rhyme effectively. It is far better to stress rhythm, meter, word choice, and the feeling and meaning to be conveyed. Not every teacher can work with poetry, but teachers who themselves like this medium should seek to share their appreciation with the class and seek a response from some members of the group. Sometimes the stories of primary children, in their naïve sharpness of imagery, approximate a form of poetry with a charm of its own. Teachers of juniors can work with the Japanese haiku if they desire form within brief compass. Here, the first line has five syllables; the second line, seven, and the last line, five, for a total of seventeen syllables.

There are various ways through which to gather the writings of a class. The classbook is sometimes used in the primary department. This is an informal gathering of written work which is mounted into pages secured together with yarn or ribbon and having a decorative cover. It could also be mimegraphed by anyone who has time to do so, so that each child would have a copy.

Fifth-graders like more elaborate ways of preserving their work and are happy to do much of it themselves. Their classbook might have a hand-blocked cover. Individual classbooks would have the mimeographed sheets put together between personally designed and constructed end papers. For a more literary flavor, they might prefer to think of their work as forming a magazine with one or two issues during the year. If they wish to write informally, a newspaper would make an appropriate format. This can be especially useful for collecting different types of learning about a series of events from biblical or church history. It provides for narrative, comment in the form of letters and editorials, poetry, and character sketches. It is a versatile form which boys and girls at this age enjoy using.

## Creative Drama

The use of drama in teaching was treated at length in Chapter 3, but it is well to note at this point that creative drama is a method by which the child can express the meaning of what he has learned. Here he must put himself in the place of the character whom he tries to convey. He must understand something of the motivation for words and actions before he can begin to imagine dialogue. Only after he has gone through this process can he go through motions which will express with any vividness what the character is trying to convey. When a class can translate a story into drama, they have demonstrated not only a knowledge of the factual material but also an understanding of the meaning behind the story.

Through creative drama the class can share its new understandings with one another, as some members take part in one scene, and others take on the role for another scene. They can share their knowledge with wider groups such as another class or department, or their parents. As a teacher watches a class at work preparing such a dramatization, it quickly becomes apparent where the lack of insight lies. The teacher might say to a child, "Why do you think he is saying these words? How does he think his words will be received? How else might he say them?" Such probing questions help the child to think more deeply about the motivations of the characters as well as their words and actions.

The only preliminary materials developed for creative drama are the sketch of the situations to be worked out and the description of the characters involved. The conversation is built up as different groups of children try out the roles and come to a consensus of what they are trying to convey. When this conversation has neared a final form, the material may be tape-recorded and played back (if you are working at this intensively) so that they can hear themselves. A recording of the final performance may then be typed up and mimeographed so that each may have a copy. At no point, however, should the children have lines to read, not even their own lines. It must be oral interpretation at every point.

## Musical Forms as Communication

Those who enjoy music feel that no other form of expression has the same power for emotional impact. Whether one is to weep or to laugh, to feel depressed or heroic, to be delighted or to be stirred up—music is the vehicle par excellence.

The church can provide boys and girls ample opportunity to learn the meaning of the biblical faith through music, in hymns, cantatas, spirituals, and other forms of religious music. If we make full use of this opportunity, some of them will be able to express their own understandings through music. Admittedly, this form of creative expression will have most appeal to teachers who find meaning in music, and the purpose of this section is to encourage teachers who are musically inclined. Children do express themselves in musical form, but they need to be encouraged to do so. Even the planned use of bells, drums, and cymbals (as accompaniment, say, for Psalm 150) would be a form of musical expression. A simple chant could be used to convey the response to a litany by boys and girls who have composed one. Pupils who want to try musical expression will be helped by listening to both plainsong and contemporary music. These, like modern poetry, do not strive for strict use of time or always harmonious modulations. To be sure, modern music is carefully constructed, and without a technical knowledge of theory and composition, no one is going to produce music on a professional level. But small children, particularly, like to put their thoughts into melody and this can be captured for the expression of religious response. The occasional child who has a gift for melody will be encouraged to have his response used by the junior choir or by the whole class in a period of worship.

## Constructive Activities

One cannot make a hard-and-fast differentiation between creative and constructive forms except in some obvious areas. What one does with paint on a blank sheet of paper or how one uses a lump of clay bring about creative changes which must first be seen in the mind of the person who works. At their best, the constructive projects involve a similar use of imagination. While creative forms should be used to express the meaning and significance of learning, the constructive forms are more often used to indicate the facts learned. Many children can happily express the latter but find great difficulty in pressing toward the former goal.

Older boys and girls are enabled to grasp the geography

of an area of study through a map which they make. The map could be drawn on the chalkboard with colored chalk by several children who continue the activity over a period of weeks and explain their work to the group. Three-dimensional maps which help them to visualize the kind of land can be made of clay or a salt and flour mixture (equal parts of salt and flour moistened slightly with water). This may be painted to show water, mountain, plain and desert. Individual flat maps can form material to be kept in an individual notebook or folio for the year's study. Background material for such maps comes from a filmstrip, an atlas, or a photographic picture book of land and people. Map-making becomes both a basis for biblical study and an illustration of such study.

The time-line is used to help fifth- and sixth-graders begin to grasp the centuries involved in biblical study and in church history. It can take the form of a long chart in which centuries are lined out as on a ruler, and key events are designated by pictures (either drawings or cutouts). A time-line may also be literally a line, a string stretched across the wall, with centuries designated by symbols clipped into place at appropriate intervals.

Charts of various kinds are ways in which a class can both express and strengthen learning. Most classes have one or more pupils who do excellent printing (and others who would rather not even try to print). Let the good printers take their time preparing the necessary printing on a large poster concerning the Ten Commandments, the Creed, a psalm, a hymn, or a set of class rules. Others can illustrate the poster with drawings or cutouts. Thus a class activity becomes both a reinforcement of learning and a continuing reminder of material learned. Tables listing the main events of Old Testament history, the life of Christ, or the history of the church can be made by the class.

Another way in which the facts of the material learned, as well as its meaning, can be indicated is through the use of tests and quizzes. Boys and girls enjoy such tests when there is a minimum of pressure on them, when they are not marked or graded, except "for fun." Tests should have the informality of the quizzes which appear in popular magazines: "If you get ten right you've nothing more to learn; if your score is seven, you've made it; if you could only think of five—better study some more." Such quizzes can take several forms: true-false, completion (fill in the correct word or phrase), matching answers from two columns, or choosing the correct word from among several to fill in a space.

Beginning with fourth grade you can use the kind of test which requires more writing and which will encourage the child to express meaning as well as facts. This might take the form of completing a paragraph (twenty-five words), such as: Moses was a faithful leader of God's people because . . . Another might be "He who would be greatest among you must be your servant" means . . . You could also ask for a summary report: Last week we talked about the prophet Isaiah. What did we say?

Children in the first few grades are not ready to write out this kind of answer, but will respond to an oral quiz. This could take the form of a guessing game: "I am thinking of a prophet who . . ."; "I am thinking of the part of the church where . . ." Children also like to make up questions to ask of one another.

It is important to remember that theological language is not taught in public school. Definitions and spelling of special words are something which boys and girls will have to learn in church school or not at all. An occasional spelling bee with the fourth-graders would not be amiss. Another learning game divides the class into groups to explain or define names, places and terms.

## Constructive Activity in Visual Form

Here the teacher usually thinks first of two-dimensional forms. A large sheet of paper or cardboard and a selection of small pictures to be trimmed suggests the making of a poster. This might illustrate signs of spring, ways we show thankfulness, or family activities. Colored papers or strips of material suggest backgrounds for the pictures or materials for the key words in the poster. Cutout figures provide more versatility, since they can be combined to form one scene. Overlapping materials will suggest depth: a person standing against a tree, for example. It is not necessary that figures be drawn first; free cutting and even free tearing of figures is often more effective because it produces less stilted forms.

When there is a continued story or a series of incidents to be retold, children have often used the technique of a movie or show. This consists of a series of individual pictures pasted together to form a long roll. The roll is mounted on rounded poles fastened at each end, inserted at the top and bottom of a cardboard carton. One flat surface of the carton is cut out to provide the screen. Then the story can be unrolled and told with pictures. The Kabachi screen is similarly made, but the pictures are kept separate, and are painted on a fairly stiff surface such as oaktag. As each incident is told, the picture is removed to the back of the series.

126

Stained-glass window designs are another type of two-dimensional picture. A large black sheet of construction paper forms the background. Sections are cut out and colored paper inserted for the stained-glass effect. (A large sheet of wrapping paper could be used and the framework colored black). In its simplest form, the children merely use crayons on this paper to make their pictures. Cellophane paper, although somewhat difficult to handle, can be used by older children in a window depicting symbols. Methods of ironing crayoned colors into the paper to get a translucent effect need special handling. A few drops of oil on the paper can make it transparent, but oily! Experiment at home.

Mosaic pictures are a form of slightly raised picture. This is an imitation, using paper squares, of a form of art used in the early Byzantine period of the church. Paper mosaics are more effectively done by the use of pre-glued papers. First the basic design or picture is made from the small squares; then the outline on the background paper is filled in.

The use of seed mosaics is more elaborate, but can be a fascinating project. A basic outline is drawn on cardboard and then filled in by the use of various materials such as dried beans of differing types and colors, rice, and small macaroni. (A pair of tweezers is a useful tool, and muffin tins can hold a variety of seeds.) Glue is the binder. When the basic design has been outlined, the entire background area is spread with glue and covered with a fine material, such as salt or sand. The next day the finished piece can be sprayed with clear plastic or enamel.

Making sand mosaics, an old craft, is based on the use of multicolored sand. Most sixth-graders would enjoy most forms of mosaics, for these are difficult enough to be challenging to their skills, and require sufficient care to give them the satisfaction of having made something important.

Printing methods of various kinds are also useful. Basically these are used for designs, although any type of figure may be printed. The linoleum block is the standard form, and can be used with fifth-graders under guidance. Potato prints are simpler, but since they involve the use of tools, they should also be done only with a small group at a time under guidance. Cardboard prints are a possibility for younger children, since these consist only of a raised cardboard figure glued to another piece of cardboard. This device needs a little practice by the teacher before he uses it in class. In each case ink, or an ink pad, is used to transfer the design to the material being printed.

Prints can be used to accentuate a poster, to make a notebook cover, to make greeting cards, or to imprint a cloth hanging that can be used as decoration in a room.

Cloth is used as the background material for sewing projects. A fourth-grade class whose teacher had an interest in stitching chose a biblical story, outlined the figures on white muslin, and then cut out figures from colored cloth. These were pinned and then stitched into place on the muslin, to make an effective appliqué. The wall hanging formed a reminder of their study.

A three-dimensional poster can be made by standing figures out from the surface of board or cardboard. Effective forms of such paper work are often seen in store window displays. Actual three-dimensional materials may also be used: pieces of wood, sponge, plant material, or small objects.

The scene or diorama is more completely three-dimensional. It can be as simple or as elaborate as the skills and interest of class and teacher would indicate. The faithfulness with which a class works at trying to make the scene authentic is an indication of the carefulness with which they have learned. A family desert camp should reflect the kind of life the patriarchs and the people in their wilderness journeys knew: the tent, the well, the flocks, the trees, the dress. The Palestine village, first-century style, needs flat-roofed houses and a village center. A box scene is more constricted in its scale, a sort of miniature stage setting. It is used for retelling a story. Many children have seen dioramas in a museum so they know what one should look like, although the techniques used in making a diorama in a church school class will be simpler.

Two processes should be mentioned which are used in a variety of ways. One is spatter-printing. A sheet of paper is placed in a box and a cardboard outline figure placed over the paper. A wire screen covers the box and colored ink is rubbed through the screen with a brush. The ink spatters and outlines the figure. This method of operation is suggested because the box keeps the ink to a limited area. Various kinds of spray cans available can also be used for spatter-painting directly on the outlines of the figure. Spatter-painting is used for notebook work and posters, and on paper, cardboard, or cloth. Spray paints should be used in ventilated areas. It is surprising how far spray paint can drift.

Blueprinting is a process often used with plant material. It consists in placing in sunlight a piece of blueprint paper on which a leaf or other plant is laid. This is covered by a piece of glass. After about a five-minute exposure to strong sunlight, the blueprint paper is dipped in a solution and allowed to dry in the shade. It will then be found to bear the print of the plant. Children enjoy the seeming mystery of the process and its careful order of procedure. They like having a "professional" piece of work when finished. Blueprints can be used on book covers or posters.

The use of a collection should be mentioned as a way of correlating and indicating knowledge. The wonder of God's creation is exhibited in shells, stones, or plants. The knowledge of a particular biblical or historical period is built up by keeping a table or shelf on which are placed objects suggestive of the time. The understanding of people in the church in some distant part of the world is encouraged as children bring to share with others (or make in class) objects familiar to that place.

Our place in God's world is suggested when children can have the opportunity of caring for growing things. This might involve a fishbowl, some tadpoles, a frog, or snails. The children could watch a cocoon open (especially in vacation church school, where they are likely to be present on the crucial day). They can grow plants or plant seeds (in cotton or in soil), plant bulbs in water or pebbles, or develop a simple outdoor garden. These are important ways to help them to realize the slowness of the growing process, the fact that each thing grows in its own way and in its own time, and the specific ways in which we help or hinder the process.

Children who live in winter climates can set up a bird-feeding station and watch the visitors who approach outside their window. In the spring they might set up a piece of screening in which are invitingly placed nest-building materials such as dried grass, straw, rootlets, feathers, cotton, string, bright pieces of ribbon and yarn, wood chips, and shavings. The birds will come to help themselves. A flat pan of soft mud is useful to robins. They use this in the building of their nests.

Children in town and suburban situations who can go for a walk always enjoy the opportunity to feed the squirrels. They like to watch the creatures solemnly sitting up to investigate the peanuts thrown to them and then running off quickly and dashing up the nearest tree.

## Using New Ideas

"There are many ideas here," you say, "but how do I use them with my curriculum materials which already suggest activities for the session?"

A teacher will feel more free and comfortable in his work once he realizes that the curriculum writer is trying to keep in mind the majority of teachers. He tries to suggest activities which most churches can use. He hopes that the ideas of the teacher's guide will spark the imagination of many teachers, so that they will make adaptations in terms of their facilities, the materials and equipment available to them, the skills of the children, the time available, and their own skills. This does not mean that teachers should feel free to depart radically from suggested learning experiences. The objectives of the class session or unit are to be kept in mind and the class led toward them. The curriculum writer has chosen the methods he feels are most likely to succeed in helping the class reach the objectives. But the alert teacher will make adaptations to suit his particular classes.

Let us look at this specifically. If part of a class session is to be used in hand activity work, it will be either individual work or a group activity. Your teacher's guide suggests a group activity. You have a large class and decide to ask a mother to help so that you can divide into two groups. The construction of a poster is suggested by the guide, a fairly simple method is advanced. Now you have in your class several highly talented art pupils. You modify the suggestion, beamed at what any class can do, and decide to have your class try to make a three-dimensional poster. In making this decision, you have carried out the purpose of the curriculum writer that the class should engage in some large project by which they could act together to retell the story of the unit. But you have taken into consideration the size of your class (necessitating two groups), the possibilities of help (a mother), and the skill of your pupils.

On the other hand, a small class meeting in a circle in a large room would have to evolve still another plan. Each pupil might cut out or draw a picture, then paste it into place on the background poster which earlier has been taped to the wall. If even wall space were unavailable, you might decide that yours would have to be individual work. Thus, the "poster" would become individual 12- by 18-inch pages, gathered week by week into a folio kept for each child in the class.

No curriculum can be designed accurately for several thousand individual classes. Therefore, teachers need to be aware of some of the adaptations they can make when necessary. A teacher who really wants to use certain activities with a class can often, by ingenious thinking, find a way. A class should not have to consider the kitchen as its regular classroom, but (if the church school guarantees to leave it in good order) it could be an excellent activity room which individual classes or departments would sign up to use when they had special need for a long working surface, water, and a sink. Even the use of crayon on paper or cloth, pressed with a hot iron to release the oil and make a permanent print, can be a possibility here, for a helper could be responsible for the use of an iron. Finger painting, setting plaster, baking clay—all are possible in a kitchen.

The outdoors can be the setting, not only for gardening activities and the care of birds and animals, but for a walk with eyes and ears open for whatever the class is asked to look for in each season. One class kept close watch on a tree planted in the small entrance garden of a city church. On the first Sunday of each month they went to the church steps and looked at it. As the season changed from fall to winter to spring, the leaves turned red, then brown, and finally fell off. The tree was covered with snow, or it glistened with ice, or it turned brown with rain. Finally there came buds and green leaves. On each of these inspection Sundays, when they returned to their room, one person was chosen to draw a picture of the tree, recording the date. So they noted the passage of the seasons: "He has made everything beautiful in its time."

There is always the possibility of an extra session at someone's house, where the dining room or kitchen becomes the scene of the activities which the limited facilities in church school make possible. This always provides an informal atmosphere in which teacher and class get better acquainted, and the conversation becomes quite enlightening and revealing.

Such a setting is always helpful if the project is one of making gifts. The area of possibility here is so broad that one can only suggest the excellent books available in bookstores, or the fine articles that occasionally appear in the women's magazines. All sorts of simple skills and materials are brought into use as the children make potholders, decorate trays, stitch placemats, make salt and pepper shakers from thin metal cans, use clay, appliqué, or do simple sewing. Gifts may be for families, for shut-ins, or for children in a distant place. These represent still another aspect of the communication of the understanding of the Christian faith to others—an expression of loving kindness.

## Communication Through Actions

We ordinarily think of communication as "getting across" something which we know or have learned. On the most obvious level, a teacher knows that learning has taken place when a class is able to "give back" information in the form of notebook work, quizzes, or pictures. Understanding has deepened if the child is able to ask probing questions or make serious comments; if he is able to do original painting or writing which denotes an inner comprehension of material; if he can take a role and really dramatize a character.

Of course our church schools are limited to the amount of time each pupil spends there, and the teacher is not in a position to go through life with the child—which would not always be wise if he could. Perhaps, beyond teaching the child as effectively as possible the most we teachers can do is to try to see that the church school situation reflects, as best as we can get it to, a Christian community of love, of respect for all individuals of eagerness to help one another, to forgive, to accept.

## For Further Reading

Allstrom, Elizabeth, *Let's Play a Story*. Nashville: Abingdon, 1957.

Anderson, Vernon, *Before You Teach Children*. Philadelphia: Lutheran Church Press, 1963.

Arbuthnot, May Hill, *Time for Poetry*. Chicago: Scott-Foresman, 1952.

Benson, Kenneth R., *Creative Crafts for Children*. Englewood Cliffs, New Jersey: Prentice-Hall, 1958.

Brown, Jeanette Perkins, *The Storyteller in Religious Education: How to Tell Stories to Children and Young People*. Boston: Pilgrim Press, 1952.

Cully, Iris V., *Children in the Church*. Philadelphia: Westminster, 1960.

Gilbert, W. Kent, *As Christians Teach*. Philadelphia: Fortress Press, 1963.

Heikkinen, Jacob W., and Luebbe, Barbara M., *Helping Children Know the Bible*. Philadelphia: Lutheran Church Press, 1963.

Herzel, Catherine, *Helping Children Worship*, Lutheran Church Press, 1963.

Keiser, Armilda, *Here's How and When*. New York: Friendship Press, 1952.

Lobingier, Elizabeth M., *Activities in Child Education for the Church School Teacher*. Boston: Pilgrim Press, 1950.

Morsch, Vivian Sharp, *The Use of Music in Christian Education*. Philadelphia: Westminster, 1956.

Nathan, Walter, *Art and the Message of the Church*. Philadelphia: Westminster, 1961.

Rest, Frederich, *Our Christian Symbols*. Philadelphia: Christian Education Press, 1954.

Rice, Rebecca, *Creative Activities*. Boston: Pilgrim Press, 1947.

Rumpf, Oscar, *The Use of Audio-Visuals in the Church*. Philadelphia: Christian Education Press, 1958.

Siks, Geraldine B., *Creative Dramatics*. New York: Harper & Brothers, 1958.

Terrien, Samuel, *Lands of the Bible*. New York: Simon and Schuster, 1958.

Thomas, Edith Lovell, *Music in Christian Education through Study and Practice*. Nashville: Abingdon-Cokesbury, 1953.

Tooze, Ruth, *Storytelling*. Englewood Cliffs, New Jersey: Prentice-Hall, 1959.

Tower, Howard E., *Church Use of Audio-Visuals*. Abingdon-Cokesbury, 1951.

Ward, Winifred, *Drama with and for Children*, U. S. Department of Health, Education and Welfare, 1960.

Ward, Winifred, *Playmaking with Children, from Kindergarten through Junior High School*. 2nd ed.; New York: Appleton-Century-Crofts, Inc., 1957.

*Type,* 11 on 13 Caledonia
*Display,* Hyperion
*Paper,* Test Offset